BOGUSŁAW SCHAEFFER
AN ANTHOLOGY

BOGUSŁAW SCHAEFFER

AN ANTHOLOGY

- SCENARIO FOR A NON-EXISTING, BUT POSSIBLE INSTRUMENTAL ACTOR
- QUARTET FOR FOUR ACTORS
- SCENARIO FOR THREE ACTORS

TRANSLATED AND INTRODUCED BY
MAGDA ROMANSKA
FOREWORD BY **RICHARD DEMARCO**

OBERON BOOKS
LONDON

WWW.OBERONBOOKS.COM

First published in 2012 by Oberon Books Ltd
521 Caledonian Road, London N7 9RH
Tel: +44 (0) 20 7607 3637 / Fax: +44 (0) 20 7607 3629
e-mail: info@oberonbooks.com

PB ISBN: 978-1-84943-464-5
Digital ISBN: 978-1-84943-722-6

Cover: photo by Tytus Żmijewski
from Bogusław Schaeffer's *A Multimedia Thing*.

eBook converted
by CPI Group (UK) Ltd, Croydon, CR0 4YY.

Contents

FOREWORD

Bogusław Schaeffer personified the spirit of the Polish avant-garde in the years that followed the ending of the Second World War in Europe. In fact, he personified the spirit of avant-gardism associated with that part of Europe which was defined politically as The Eastern Bloc, that region of Europe that threatened the security of Western Europe and, indeed, what was then known as The Free World.

Despite the tragedy of this world war, and the fifty years of The Cold War which followed, the art of Bogusław Schaeffer has been appreciated and performed in The Netherlands, Italy, Belgium, Hungary, United States, Argentina, Germany, Switzerland, Denmark, Russia, Norway, France, The Czech Republic, Austria and Croatia. Although it was performed prior to 1972 in London, it has unfortunately remained virtually unknown in Scotland.

I associate Bogusław Schaeffer's contribution to international avant-gardism as belonging to the world he inherited from the avant-garde artists who lived and worked in Poland, not only during the Second World War, but in the pre-war years in the 1930s.

His lifetime's work as an avant-gardist clearly takes into account the achievements of heroic figures in the history of twentieth-century art in Poland such as Stanisław Witkiewicz, Bruno Schulz, Witold Gombrowicz and Stanisław Wyspiański. However, as the language of true art is essentially international, he also belonged to the small but vitally important group of artists who were expressing in an international arena the interface between music, theatre and the visual arts.

I first encountered the reality of Bogusław Schaeffer's art in 1972 when, in collaboration with The Muzeum Sztuki (The Art Museum) in Łódź, under the direction of Ryszard Stanisławski, and The Foksal Gallery, under the direction of Wiesław Borowski, The Demarco Gallery presented the Official Edinburgh Festival exhibition entitled 'Atelier 72'. It was part of a programme I had devised for the years 1970-1973 in order to introduce the art of what I considered as 'an imprisoned Europe' into the Official Edinburgh International Festival programme. This art was virtually obscured and unrecorded because it was physically repressed under the heel of Russian Soviet imperialism. My Official Edinburgh Festival programme, therefore, focused in 1970 on the exhibition entitled 'Strategy: Get Arts' expressing the culture of a Germany divided by The Iron Curtain.

Following this exhibition in 1971, my Festival programme was focused on Romania because Romanian intellectual and cultural initiatives had suffered the fate of being repressed by, first, Nazi Germany, and then Russian Communism, and, perhaps even worse, the dictatorship of Nicolae Ceausescu. The plight of Romania was similar to that of Poland. Therefore, in 1972 in relation to West Germany and Romania, I presented an exhibition of about seventy Polish artists entitled 'Atelier 72'.

Published in the 'Atelier 72' exhibition catalogue was a statement by Bogusław Schaeffer on his theories of what he termed at that time 'audio visual music' and 'action music'. It was obviously an attitude which could be compared to statements made by John Cage in the Sixties and Seventies, and his Danish equivalent, Henning Christiansen, a colleague of Joseph Beuys, and Joseph Beuys himself who, together with Henning Christiansen, presented a masterwork inspired by Scottish folk culture expressed through folk songs and story-telling fusing together Scottish and Irish history and mythology. Joseph Beuys entitled it *Celtic Kinloch Rannoch: The Scottish Symphony*. It was in response to Felix Mendelssohn's travels in The Western Isles of Scotland which resulted in Mendelssohn's world famous *Hebrides Overture*.

Bogusław Schaeffer's statement regarding audio-visual music was obviously at one with the audio-visual art of other German artist/composers I presented in 1970 under the aegis of 'Strategy: Get Arts'. It resonated with the music of Friedhelm Döhl, in collaboration with Günther Uecker; he presented a music-based 'action' entitled *Sound-Scene* at Edinburgh College of Art. This was performed along with the music of Mauricio Kagel through the medium of film. It was a homage to Beethoven and therefore was aptly entitled *Ludwig Van*. Bogusław Schaeffer's 1972 statement expressed clearly the music composed by such visual artists who were inspired in 1970 by the concept of audio-visual music.

Bogusław Schaeffer's statement in 1972 was as follows:

Audio-visual music is based on a composition idea of a particular kind. Compositions of this type have not as yet been given a specific name; nevertheless, they are evidently distinct from other sorts of music. They are distinct from them both in the time and circumstances of their origin and in the type of music which they represent; in the time, for these compositions could not be written before 1960; in the circumstances, for they arose in opposition to the works conventional in cast; in the type, for they go out beyond the range of instrumental and vocal music or music for magnetic tape. I introduce a special new term in music, towards music and, still further, against music.

Through 'Atelier1972', I had to emphasise the importance of Poland located in the heartland of Europe and relate Polish culture to my exhibitions of Austrian, Yugoslav, Italian and French culture which followed in 1973.

So it was in the early Seventies that I placed Bogusław Schaeffer's genius firmly at the centre of the European cultural heritage which expressed avant-gardism during my lifetime. As I was born in 1930, my life-span can be identified with the modern movements associated with The Bauhaus as an expression of experimental art school education later made manifest in Black Mountain College, the American version of The Bauhaus.

Black Mountain College provided the art world with a combination of graphic design, architecture, modern music, dance and theatre to be identified, although based in the United States, by an upsurge of creative talent emerging from the European heartland. The art of Bogusław Schaeffer would have been thoroughly 'at home' there.

The Edinburgh Festival presents the world's largest international stage for all the arts – for grand opera, classical and modern dance, theatre and all aspects of the visual arts as well as literature and music. This is the international stage where you must surely find the art of Bogusław Schaeffer, expressed in his 'graphic art' as well as in his music. With *Schaeffer's Era*, The Aurea Porta Theatre Company has managed to honour Bogusław Schaeffer in what can only be described as a 'Gesamtkunstwerk', that is a 'total art work'. It should be noted that a version of this performance was presented by Universal Arts for the 2010 Edinburgh Festival Fringe programme. *Schaeffer's Era* is a unique form of total theatre; it is an exhilarating and challenging mixture of grand opera, sculpture, circus, video and performance art. It expresses the re-awakening of the spirit of DADA. I regarded these performances in the same way that I regarded the ten performances of Joseph Beuys' *Celtic Kinloch Rannoch: The Scottish Symphony* in 1970 or Tadeusz Kantor's six performances of *The Dead Class* in 1976. Both took place at Edinburgh College of Art because I thought they both questioned the boundaries separating the visual and performing arts and, therefore, the very nature of education in Scottish art schools during the Seventies. They remain among the highlights of my personal experience of sixty-five years of The Edinburgh Festival. Naturally, I regard Bogusław Schaeffer's contribution to The Edinburgh Festival to be considered of equal importance to the upholding of those historic moments when, upon the Edinburgh Festival stage, the essence of twentieth-century contemporary art was made timeless and unforgettable.

Twenty years has passed since The Demarco Gallery introduced the music of Georges Enescu into the 1992 Edinburgh Festival. Like Bogusław Schaeffer, Enescu's music was rarely performed in Britain in the early years of the Edinburgh Festival, although it evoked the soul of a Europe that British cultural life dares not ignore.

In 1992, the music of Enescu was presented by The Demarco Gallery in collaboration with Oakham School represented by Mark Pitter, Oakham's Classics Master, and Robert Huw Morgan, Oakham's organist and choirmaster, and Jennifer Kelsey, the leader of Oakham School's orchestras. As an accomplished violinist, she performed Enescu's *Sonata No. 3 for Violin and Piano* with Robert Huw Morgan on piano. This masterly piece of music is an effective evocation of Romanian folk music and therefore the folk music of Europe. This is the kind of music which, like that of Schaeffer, could only originate from that part of Europe where the wellsprings of avant-gardism rise from older traditional values of folk culture. It must not be forgotten that Constantin Brancusi, the outstanding European modernist sculptor, was essentially endowed with the wisdom of Romanian peasant art.

Oakham School typifies those British schools which take music education seriously. Together with others, it has reassured me through many decades that art education was integral to the life of any school, whether state or private. I am never forgetful of my years as a school teacher when I was fortunate to work alongside Arthur Oldham, the founder of The Edinburgh Festival Chorus. He inspired me to think that the world of the Edinburgh Festival should not be separated from educational systems on primary and secondary levels. I am, therefore, grateful not only to Oakham School but also to Glenalmond College, Downside School, Stewart's Melville College and Scotus Academy, which have given me ample proof over many decades that art education must be taken seriously for the greater good of society. I, therefore, regard it as a moral obligation that I should introduce the music of Bogusław Schaeffer into the world of secondary school education in Britain.

That is why it is highly significant that the spirit of avant-garde music should be performed in The Tom Fleming Centre of Stewart's Melville College. It was built for the exact purpose of school education through the performing arts on a secondary level. In fact, every institution teaching or performing music should take to heart the wisdom inherent in the words of Bogusław Schaeffer when he states:

> The task of action music is not to transmit purely musical utterances, but artistic utterances in the wider sense of the word. The share of the NON-musical element is not intended to be an addition to music, but a form of utterance equivalent to it. By employing non-musical media, we can enrich music with values so far unknown to it (note that this problem could not be involved in music, even in the musical theatre, since there, music was generally subordinated to the designed dramaturgy of the whole). Music and something more than music – that is how the programme of 'action' music might be defined.

Bogusław Schaeffer also challenges all those concerned with performing music, both orchestral and choral, by stating that 'Action music should be performed in an incoherent manner, and "coherence" will appear by itself in the course of the performance'. He also says that it is important to consider the place where audio-visual music is performed. He suggests that an ideal auditorium would cause the intermingling of the audience and the performers. He advises that the audience should consist of listeners who are also spectators.

In 2012 The Aurea Porta Theatre Company will present the audio-visual art of Bogusław Schaeffer, *A Multimedia Thing*, under the aegis of The Demarco European Art Foundation for Robert McDowell's Summerhall Edinburgh Festival programme.

Richard Demarco, July 2012

INTRODUCTION

THE THEATRE OF BOGUSŁAW SCHAEFFER

Polish theatre has gained world renown thanks to its innovative and bold experimental style. In international theatre circles, it is often enough to mention the names of Grotowski, Kantor, Witkacy, and Gombrowicz to elicit eager nods of approval. One aspect of Polish theatre that is well-known but rarely analyzed is that its great often straddle many artistic disciplines. Kantor was both painter and theatre director, Witkacy was both painter and playwright, Gombrowicz wrote novels and plays with equal ease. Drawing on that strength, Polish artists often blend many art forms, feeling equally at home in a variety of fields and genres. Poland's current most-renowned Renaissance man is Bogusław Julian Schaeffer, a playwright, composer, theoretician, and graphic designer. In 1999, to celebrate Schaeffer's 70th birthday, Jagiellonian University in Cracow organized a symposium devoted to his work. The body of speakers ranged from actors and theatre critics to musicologists and composers. Schaeffer has created 550 musical works in 23 different musical genres, written 46 plays (translated into 17 languages, including Estonian, Hungarian, and Hebrew), of which 33 have been staged in Poland – some running for 20 to 30 years – and designed about 400 graphic works. Widely regarded as a pioneer of "new music" and avant-garde theatre, Schaeffer is one of Poland's most influential contemporary composers and the most frequently performed playwright in Poland today. The recipient of wide-ranging tributes, Schaeffer is as revered as he is prolific. His *Klavier Konzert* was featured on the soundtrack to David Lynch's *Inland Empire*; Eugène Ionesco wrote *Three Dreams* in Schaeffer's honor. *Solo*, a 2008 documentary film about Schaeffer, won the Grand Prix for art film at the 2009 Montreal Film Festival, for showing "an unusual journey to the roots of an even more unusual art." In 2010, the film was screened at the National Gallery of Art in Washington, D.C., the Museum of Fine Arts in Boston, and the Morgan Library and Museum in New York. In 2009 a chocolate was created in Schaeffer's honor by Meister Hacker of Konditorei Confiserie Hacker in Rattenberg, Austria.

Schaeffer is also the only composer in Western history to have an independent dramaturgical career, and the only playwright to have an independent career as a composer. In fact, in music circles he is often known only as a composer, and in theatre circles, only as a playwright. It is often thought that having two independent professions disrupts both of them, but this is not the case with Schaeffer. On the contrary, it seems that his experience as a composer only adds originality to his playwriting and, similarly, that his experience as a playwright adds to his music career (Sugiera and Zając 1999: 7). As a theoretician in new music Schaeffer has written several books, including *New Music: Problems of Contemporary Composing Techniques*; *Small Guidebook of Twentieth-Century Music*; *Twentieth-Century Music: Creators and Problems*; *Classics of Dodecaphony*; *Introduction to Composition*; and *History of Music: Styles and Creators*. He is an author of the first handbook of modern composition (no other composer has written as many music books as he), and for a long time, he worked predominantly as a professor at the Salzburg School of Music and at the Academy of Music in Cracow. Schaeffer has held the position of Professor of Composition at the Hochschule für Musik und darstellende Kunst "Mozarteum" in Salzburg since 1985. Schaeffer wrote his first musical composition while still in high school. In 1965 he began an affiliation with the Experimental Studio of Polish Radio in Warsaw and wrote his first electronic compositions. He is the recipient of many composition competition awards. Since 1969, there have been approximately 60 concerts devoted exclusively to his works, including events in Oslo, Amsterdam, Princeton, Mexico City, Salzburg, Istanbul, Berlin, and Vienna.

Born on June 6, 1929, in Lwów, which belonged to Russia before World War II, Schaeffer learned to write at the age of five and began playing piano at the age of seven. Since his first writing attempts were discouraged by his father, whose own poetic impulses didn't bring the anticipated results, young Bogusław destroyed his writings and decided to focus on music exclusively. During the war, and while separated from his family, Schaeffer devoted himself to studying foreign languages and music theory. After the war his family reunited and settled in Opole, where Schaeffer attended the Gymnasium with a concentration in mathematics and physics. He quickly became first in his class. At the age of seventeen he wrote his first music composition, which was soon followed by 300 other short musical pieces. He became a playwright in his spare time as a respite from writing music. Writing a play, he says, comes easily compared with writing music, which is difficult. For a long time Schaeffer wrote his dramatic works in secret, keeping them from his family, and without intending ever to stage them.

His first play, written in 1955 at the age of 26, is a 28-scene opus based on the life of the Austrian composer Anton von Webern (1883–1945). A student of Schoenberg, Webern was a discriminating composer whose musical talents were not always appreciated by his contemporaries. Audiences found his music incomprehensible for the most part, and musicians often refused to perform his compositions because they considered them too difficult. In 1945 Webern was accidentally shot dead by a US soldier in the US-occupied zone; by then he had practically been sentenced to obscurity, leaving behind barely more than three hours of performable music. Webern's influence, however, flourished after World War II, inspiring many contemporary composers with his use of serialism and his emphasis on a single note. Schaeffer's play, entitled simply *Webern*, deals with the composer's position as an underappreciated artist forced to face his own unpopularity. Tracing Webern's psychological processes on the ladder to success, or failure, Schaeffer constructs a portrait of a man whose only point of reference and meaning is himself and his own conviction in the strength of his work. Though the two men were drastically different in their musical styles and personalities, Weber was at twenty-six years old Schaeffer's alter ego. *Webern* was never performed, and despite lively interest in the play in Poland, Schaeffer never attempted to have it staged. Followed by forty-five other plays written over a span of more than fifty years, *Webern* established some of the leading themes in Schaeffer's later dramaturgy: the musical form, the absurd dialog, the characters thrown into antagonistic social and political circumstances, and uniquely Schaefferian metatheatricality.

Although some of Schaeffer's plays have been performed in theatres across Poland consistently since the mid-1950s, they long remained the domain of artistic circles, objects of intellectual debates and theatrical experiments, coming to full prominence only after 1989. Following the Round Table talks that basically ended the forty-year communist regime, the Polish theatre – always entangled in one way or another in the political struggle – was suddenly left in an ideological vacuum. During the communist era, theatre in Poland held enormous political power. As a live performance, it was the only medium – unlike radio and TV – that could escape the government's censorship. Playwrights and actors learned to speak between the lines, using metaphors, symbols, or sometimes just a wink of the eye to communicate their anti-establishment sentiments to their audiences. Theatre was a subversive affair; audiences and actors, united in their common understanding of the country's political predicament, exercised the only possible form of resistance: intellectual distance from an oppressive ideology. Peter Sloterdijk called it Kynicism, "a rejection of the official culture by means of irony and sarcasm" (quoted in Žižek 1989: 29), a peculiar form of "pissing against the idealist wind," idealism in this case representing the ideological façade of the communist regime. For more than four decades, the kynical language established the lines of communication between actors and their audiences. Spectators, for their part, learned to read between the lines, interpreting everything they possibly could as a political statement. For example, in his seminal book, *Shakespeare, Our Contemporary*, Jan Kott recalls that in 1956, during a production of *Hamlet* staged only a few weeks after the Twentieth Soviet Communist Party Congress uncovered Stalin's atrocities, nobody had any doubts what the lines "Something is rotten in the state of Denmark" and "Denmark's a prison" referred to (59). In 1956 Poland they certainly weren't referring to Hamlet's Denmark. The lines at the time gained an ironic undertone and became practically a part of colloquial vocabulary as a code phrase for the Soviet state. In the same spirit, the 1967 production of Adam Mickiewicz's *Forefather's Eve*, a national romantic drama dealing with the eighteenth-century Russian partition of Poland, provoked street demonstrations and a string of subsequent persecutions of Poland's intelligentsia, writers, students, and university professors, forcing some of them into permanent exile. The year 1989 brought the fall of the Berlin Wall and, along with it, the censorship that had been an integral part of the Polish theatrical experience. Suddenly, one could say anything to anyone out loud, and there was no longer any reason to go to the theatre. The unexpected onslaught of political freedom, ironically, deprived the theatrical experience of what for forty years had been essential to it: its political subtext. The change of climate in Eastern Europe created an atmosphere in which theatre's role as the only oasis of free speech evaporated. At the same time, with the economic turnover to the free market, the state sponsorship of theatres became limited, leaving most of them to their own devices as far as funding was concerned.

It was at this point of ideological vacuum and financial shortage that Schaeffer's plays entered the Polish mainstream. Indeed, struggling with the new economic and political reality of emerging capitalism, Polish audiences, trapped in the moral, political, and socioeconomic limbo of the post-communist era, found in Schaeffer the most acute commentator of their transitory existence. Reflecting the paradoxes of newly found freedom, Schaeffer's plays probed modern power struggles, consumer culture, and the alienation of the individual trapped in their midst. In a way, Schaeffer did for Polish theatre what Roman Polanski did for Polish film: he liberated it from what Tadeusz Konwicki calls "the Polish complex" (*The Polish Complex*, 1998). Polanski's *Knife in the Water*, a 1963 short black-and-white film about a love triangle, was the first postwar Polish film that didn't deal at all with World War II, or any other national issue, for that matter. It was also the first film that could be easily understood, in its entirety, by somebody without at least a minor background in Polish history. In the same manner, Schaeffer's plays, focusing as much on form as they do on content, are practically devoid of references to Polish national themes, Polish politics, or Polish history. One can understand Schaeffer's jokes without knowing the quirks and absurdities of life under the communist regime. And indeed, faced with the new economic and political reality of burgeoning capitalism, Polish audiences found in Schaeffer the most acute commentator on the quirks and absurdities of life under capitalism. In fact, Schaeffer became so popular that various cities started organizing so-called Schaefferiads – marathons of his plays, performed by various theatres in the space of a few days.

In his short essay on Schaeffer, S. Stabro (2003) notices that Schaeffer's popularity in the 1990s was marked by the exhaustion of political language in drama, and by the return to Witkacy's concept of theatre of the "pure form." Giving up traditional dramatic elements and focusing on material aspects of theatre, Schaeffer draws not only from music but also from both *commedia dell'arte* and carnival. Moving away from theatre 'as a high art' towards its more plebian origins, Schaeffer is interested in language as a material, used for language games and as a means to parody the grand national dramatic models (Wyspiański's *Wesele* [Marriage] comes to mind) (Stabro 2003: 179). Deconstructing the pathos of Wyspiański's dramas, Schaeffer is perhaps Poland's best example of the postmodernist slant, one that "grew out of the proclamations about 'the end of art' as well as the requirements of the free market. It is theatre liberated from the modernist belief in the power of art, theatre liberated from any ambitions – naturally besides the ambition of being theatre. It is theatre open to free-flowing games with itself, its own theatrical nature" (Tytkowska 1999: 1973). Another critic, Ewa Piotrowska (1992), noted that in the 1980s,

> the ethos of theatre revolved around the mythic, Romantic and national themes; the role of the avant-garde was to portray the moral dilemmas of the generation that survived World War II and lived under the communist oppression. Theatre and actor were an instrument of the discourse about matters of national importance. With Schaeffer, we see a new tendency. [...] Today's art – with the advent of free speech – doesn't have to be either "for" or "against" anything, whether implicitly or explicitly. Thus, theatre searches for new emotions, new fascination, new real contact with the audience. Let's hope that banality and triviality is only a temporary stage, and soon enough we will return to true art that would speak of human value, not humanity, the moment, not eternity, concrete, not universal experience. Just like in [Schaeffer's work]. (122)

Blending grotesque situations, absurd language, and dark humor, Schaeffer's plays probe questions of power, sexuality, blind consumerism, elitism, and contemporary alienation. The metatheatrical theme tells the story of an actor and the theatre, but it also tells the story of life in a world in which in order to survive one must constantly assume brand-new masks and brand-new poses. Losing themselves between their desperation and their lack of a coherent self-image, Schaeffer's heroes suffer from what Bernard Rosen called the "chameleon personality." "[Schaeffer's] hero is often a Multiindividuum, [...] undergoing various metamorphoses, and unrecognizable under various masks. The artificiality of the names signifies the artificiality of their being. They are the abstract elements of preexisting *a priori* structure. [...] What's important is not what the actor says but the order in which he says it" (as quoted in Karasińska 1999: 47). The fiction and reality of the stage constantly intertwine, suspending the heroes and the viewers in a no-man's-land of ambiguous values and questionable intentions. In the confused Poland of the 1990s, Schaeffer's plays, always bringing in a paying audience, reflected the emotional and social conditions of the people, both the older generation of post-World War II baby boomers who, thrust into a new economic reality and often unable to adjust, came to be tragically described by sociologists as the "lost generation," and the young, who had already forgotten the long breadlines of the communist era but were not yet able to grasp the mechanisms of the capitalist market. The transitional 1990s became Schaeffer's decade on the Polish stage in every sense of the word.

As a composer of music, Schaeffer is what we might call a conceptual composer, in the lineage of Mauricio Kagel, Karlheinz Stockhausen, Ernest Austin, and John Cage. His microtonal compositions are carefully structured and employ cyclical repetitions, and codes. Schaeffer's dramas share similar characteristics: cyclical repetitions, episodic arrangements, and mathematical precision in their dramatic structure. Jerzy Popiela called the particularity of Schaeffer's dramatic structure "Schaefferismo," a term borrowed from music, and in Schaeffer's case, delineating a specific conceptual metatheatricality (as cited in Zając 1998: 81). Joanna Zając (1998) called Schaeffer's dramas an example of the Instrumental Theatre, a term also borrowed from musicology (86). Used interchangeably with the term "spatial music," the term Instrumental Theatre refers to various experiments with moving sound. Alexander Scriabin, a turn-of-the-century Russian symbolist composer, was the first to conceive the idea of sound movement. Scriabin's experiments were part of a larger avant-garde trend of that time that favored experiments with movement, sound, and image, and that included Meyerhold's bio-mechanics, Schlemmer's mechanical ballets, and Foregger's constructivist dance workshops. After Scriabin, Mauricio Kagel, an Argentine composer born in 1931 who worked predominantly in Germany, was the one who actually defined the concept of the Instrumental Theatre and who utilized its principles in his work. According to Kagel, in Instrumental Theatre the movement of sound must undergo constant and unexpected changes. The actions of the musician-performers are thus as important as the sounds they make. The origins of Kagel's work can be found in Expressionism, Surrealism, and Dadaism, but he was also influenced by Brecht's theory of distantiation and Beckett's theatrical experiments with sound, time, and space.

It was that quest for "new realms of sonic and bodily expressions that led Schaeffer to experimenting with the theatre and actors, and to examining of the influence that the bodily presence of the performers has upon the public" (Caprioli 1999: 117). Following some of Kagel's experiments with sound movement, Schaeffer has created a unique theatrical language in which the actor is viewed as an "instrumental medium" (Zając 1998: 81). The text sometimes suggests that actors can choose between different theatrical selves. "Text turns into an impulse for physical action. Sometimes the actor's body is reduced to a sign or a symbol. Sometimes, one gesture or a movement can become a metaphor" (Zając 1998: 138). Thus, the actors are constantly aware of the structural framework of each play and the relationship between text, movement, and sound. "The instrumental actor treats himself with a distance, like an instrument. Like an object or a medium, which can only become a work of art. The actor sees himself from the outside, like a sculptor looking at a matter at hand" (Zając 1998: 157). In this arrangement, Schaeffer conducts his actors as he does his musicians. Yet, Schaeffer is "more interested in the creation of homogenous new motives than in the construction of musical or theatrical structures. His works are contemporary collages, hardly yielding to the rules of interpretative logic" (Zajac 1999: 25).

Schaeffer's first instrumental play included actors, musicians, and dancers. Written in 1963, *TIS MW2 dla aktora, mima, tancerki i 5 muzyków* (*Tis MW2 for an Actor, Mime, Dancers and Five Musicians*), as the title implies, combined quasi-theatrical and quasi-instrumental elements. *TIS* itself stood for Instrumental Theatre of Schaeffer (Teatr Instrumentaly Schaeffera). *MW2* stood for Young Performers of Contemporary Music (Młodzi Wykonawcy Muzyki Współczesnej). At that time, Schaeffer was interested not in a new form of theatre but rather in music as performed by actors and dancers. Lead by Adam Kaczyński, MW2 had ambitions to perform the classics of decaphonic music, including among others Weber's, as well as new experimental works. *TIS MW2* was inspired by the modernist novel *Pałuba* (1903), by the Polish writer Karol Irzykowski. The novel consists of two complementary parts: the fictional biography of Piotr Strumieński and an analytical commentary of the author on the very process of writing it. *Pałuba* is considered the first Polish self-referential novel; it analyzes juxtaposing modes of life: ideals vs. the pragmatic, constructivist necessities of living. Schaeffer read *Pałuba* a number of times, dividing it into fragments and segments. Likewise, *TIS MW2* has an episodic composition; it is divided into segments, performed sequentially. Each segment would later became the basis for Schaeffer's other dramatic compositions. The performance opened on April 24, 1964, with Adam Kaczyński and Mark Mietelski playing piano, Marian Lata playing saxophone, and Barbara Świątek playing flute. Besides musicians, the group also included a dancer, Krystna Ungeheuer, and actors, Bogusław Kierc and Jan Peszek. In the first ten years, the show was performed over thirty times in various cities across Europe, including Istanbul. The performance followed Kagel's premise for Instrumental Theatre, with one exception: instead of musicians, Schaeffer used professional actors. *TIS MW2* became Schaeffer's transitional piece, in which he moved from music to theatre. From then on, his dramatic works as well as his musical works continued to straddle the thin line between the two arts.

Scenario for a Non-Existing, but Possible Instrumental Actor (*Scenariusz dla nie istniejącego lecz możliwego aktora instrumentalnego*) was Schaeffer's next project. It provides an excellent sampling of Schaeffer's stylistic range, as it includes monologue, poetry, dialogue, and musical/linguistic arrangements. It is also his longest-running performance piece. It was written in 1963, but it didn't open until 1976, in Cracow, under the patronage of the group MW2, and with Jan Peszek, by then one of Poland's leading actors, in the title role. Schaeffer and Peszek met in Cracow, while Peszek was still a student at The Ludwig Solski State Drama School in Cracow (PWST). He played the part of the "actor without a text" in Schaeffer's *TIS MW2*. At that time, Peszek recalls, he didn't know anything about the Instrumental Theatre, or about the idea behind it. He was also completely unaware of what it meant to be an Instrumental actor. Schaeffer wrote the *Scenario* specifically for Peszek, although Peszek initially resisted Schaeffer's offer to perform it, as it seemed to him better suited to an academic lecture on contemporary art than to a theatre performance. Eventually, after being pestered by Schaeffer for a few months, Peszek began to read and reread the text from the point of view of Charles, the main character's vulgar friend with aspirations to gentility. It took Schaeffer and Peszek eleven years to officially open the show.

Rehearsing the *Scenario,* Peszek eventually realized that "serious issues related to the crisis of art can be presented on stage only within the poetics of the grotesque" (Peszek 1999: 191). Inspired by Georg Simmel, the early-twentieth-century German philosopher and sociologist, Peszek began exploring what Simmel called "the third zone," an autonomous sphere between true reality ("aesthetic naturalism"), and dramatic fiction (the "ideals"). In his essay "Zur Philosophie des Schauspielers" (1908, "On the Philosophy of the Actor"), Simmel discusses how the two interpretative schools of acting provide false senses of the acting process (as cited in Wolff 1964: xliii n11). The first school, that of "aesthetic naturalism," aims to portray the role the way that a real Hamlet, for example, would behave had he actually existed and ruled Denmark. The second trend, which promotes the ideal conception of a dramatic role, suggests that the dramatic realization of the character of Hamlet could be derived only from Shakespeare's text of the play, without any experiential explorations. Guy Oakes, in his 1980 introduction to Simmel's *Essays on Interpretation in Social*

Science, wrote that "The first view entails that acting as a form is reducible to the form of reality. The second view entails that acting is reducible to the form of drama. Both theses entail that there is ultimately only one legitimate interpretation of a given dramatic role, one idea and uniquely authentic conception which the actor may approximate more or less closely" (74–75). True acting, Simmel argues, takes places in the "third zone," which is located in between the other two: it blends the experiential and the textual into an interpretative mode that enhances the actor's (and our) understanding of reality. Simmel further argues that in his exploration of the text and the social situation it describes, the actor follows the process of *Verstehen*, an "interpretive or participatory examination" of social phenomena. The concept of *Verstehen* (lit. "understanding") was initially described by Wilhelm Dilthey, the late-nineteenth-century German historian and philosopher, and introduced into sociology and anthropology by Max Weber and Simmel. Simmel, however, was the first to use it in reference to theatre.

Working with Schaeffer's text, Peszek discovered that the "third zone" also exists in his dramas; this is possible because Schaeffer's dramas are engaged with the issues of the drama as such. This is particularly true for the *Scenario,* which focuses on the role and function of art in the contemporary world. In Schaeffer's dramatic structure, all the stage elements (acting, design, music, etc.) blend into one another, leading to tensions and antinomies. Thus, Schaeffer's actor necessarily becomes "aware that all in all every scenic role is not a straight line but an assortment of disjointed elements" (Peszek 1999: 192). Schaeffer was, according to Peszek, the fist person to make him aware of the role of the actor's voice as a separate element of the production.

The *Scenario* is based on Walter Benjamin's famous essay "The Work of Art in the Age of Mechanical Reproduction." Benjamin, a philosopher and cultural theorist, argues that technology, particularly easy mechanical reproduction, diminishes the "aura" of art objects, dissolving their ritualistic aspect and erasing the very notion of "authenticity." Benjamin defines the 'aura of the work of art' as "that which withers in the age of mechanical reproduction" (1935/1988: 211). Mechanical reproduction strips the work of art of its aura because it "substitutes a plurality of copies for a unique existence" (211). The aura, Benjamin argues, is inevitably connected to the ritualistic, religious aspect of the work of art:

> Originally the contextual integration of art in tradition found its expression in the cult. We know that the earliest art works originated in the service of a ritual – first the magical, then the religious kind. It is significant that the existence of the work of art with reference to its aura is never entirely separated from its ritual function. In other words, the unique value of the "authentic" work of art has its basis in ritual, the location of its original use value. (223–24)

Benjamin separates film from theatre, arguing that the theatrical event preserves the aura, while the cinematic one destroys it. Film is easily available and reproducible, whereas the theatrical experience, by necessity, is singular and of limited availability. Benjamin writes:

> The aura which, on the stage, emanates from Macbeth, cannot be separated for the spectators from that of the actor. However, the singularity of the shot in the studio is that the camera is substituted for the public. Consequently, the aura that envelops the actor vanishes, and with it the aura of the figure he portrays. (229)

Following Benjamin's divagations, the *Scenario* addresses poststructuralist concepts of authorship and loss of creative agency in a postmodern world of fluid, ambivalent values. Its hero attempts to determine the intrinsic worth of art (besides its material consumption) and whether it can at all be defined and measured. Art, he seems to suggest, is a drive, independent of social and economic conventions – a drive to respond to them, but not be of them. The performance starts with Peszek, dressed in a suit, lecturing; his tone of voice is pompous and professorial. Soon enough, however, his performance disintegrates as he begins to eat an apple, to jump around, and to mix flour with water, all while continuing to recite his lines. At some point, Peszek hangs upside down on a ladder, eating an apple, and continues the lecture without batting an eye. (In another moment, the actor – playing Charlie – pees on the stage. In that scene, Peszek uses an aluminum can to simulate the sound of peeing.) Here's how theatre critic Leszek Pulka (2003) describes the play:

> We have to assume that Schaeffer wrote a "dada" kind of text meant for an equilibrist performer. The performer attacks the audience with the most serious statements about contemporary art while climbing a ladder, swinging buckets, taming an invisible stallion or juggling. By juxtaposing crucial philosophical statements with inane physical activity he questions the limits of art. He also explores the financial, artistic and social limits of independence. [...] He draws his audience into hysterics when, standing at a table awkwardly mixing flour and water by hand, he explains the details of Heidegger's philosophy or, rubbing his eye, he ponders eternal values.

Thus, in Peszek's interpretation, the *Scenario* becomes a grotesque circus performance, in which Peszek's voice, body, and face become instruments of expression – like other musical instruments. The *Scenario* is also in a way a musical work, as the main hero leads the viewers through the trials and tribulations of contemporary music, citing examples and its development, both using his body and surrounding himself with props and set.

The structure of the *Scenario* follows the typical lecture; however, the subject matter seems to overwhelm the performer, who breaks the flow, diverges from his main topic, and wanders off into various directions, driven mad by the problems he tries to analyze. The grotesque juxtaposition between the pathos of the text and its circus-like performance is jarring and funny at the same time: perhaps it is funny because it is jarring, making us aware how seriously unserious our serious discourse is, or perhaps vice versa, how unserious our serious discourse has become. The laughter at the expense of that juxtaposition, as Sylwia Lichocka (2010) notes, is problematic because in some sense it does preclude the connection between the artist and his audience. When it first opened, some critics considered it an inside joke of the avant-garde – a kind of spoof on itself, making a point that the artist's role is to be both priest and clown. This approach follows the typical motive in Polish culture, a "dialectic of apotheosis and derision," whereas art is elevated to a near-mystical status, while simultaneously being mocked and derided for what it's offering its followers: a marginal life of poverty and isolation. In Schaeffer's hands, art becomes both holy and profane. The show is also a form of challenge: the actor promises to keep our attention for over an hour while reciting an academic lecture on art. In doing so, he makes a point that in principle negates the very lecture: art does have power. It is this in-between-ness, the liminal quality of the spectacle, that perhaps is most captivating: Peszek balances between text and stage, reality and illusion, constantly both asserting and negating his own theses.

Since its premiere in 1976, the *Scenario* has been staged over 1,500 times around the world. Besides theatres, the show has been performed in such unusual locations as barns, mine pits, airports, basements, and castles. In 1988, it was filmed by Polish Television Theatre. During its forty-year run, the *Scenario* has been critically acclaimed and has won many awards, including the 1995 Grand Prix at New York's Theatre Festival. Eventually, Jan Peszek handed the script over to the young French actor André Erlen. Born in 1974, Erlen graduated from Kunstakademie Düsseldorf. From 1991 to 2001, he was a member of Actors' Studio Pulheim, performing with the ensemble in such productions as *The Marriage* by W. Gombrowicz, *Woyzek* by G. Büchner, and *Emigrants* by S. Mrozek. Erlen's version of the *Scenario*, performed in German, was directed by Peszek himself and it opened in 2002 at Düsseldorfer Schauspielhaus and at Teatr Groteska in Cracow. As Peszek put it in one of his interviews, the idea of handing over the script came from the Japanese tradition of passing a role from an older to a younger actor. Peszek, however, continues to perform his *Scenario*. In 2011, when asked whether he's bored, he replied: "My hero is not bored at all, particularly now, when times have changed and they're especially frustrating for the artists. I'd say more, we became friends of a sort" (Peszek, quoted in JOC 2011).

The Quartet for Four Actors (*Kwartet na czterech aktorów*) was Schaeffer's first full-length instrumental play. It is derived from Schaeffer's 1966 text written for MW2. This first version was mostly based on improvisation. It also used fragments of Ionesco's text *Three Dreams About Schaeffer*, which Ionesco wrote in Schaeffer's honor. Ionesco's text is a short microdrama in three parts about a man who tries to control his life: each part is a variation on the same theme. In 1972, Schaeffer composed

26

a musical piece based on the same Ionesco's text. The full production of *Quartet* opened on February 24, 1979, at Teatr im. Stefana Jaracza in Łódź under the direction of Mikołaj Grabowski, with Jacek Chmielik, Wojciech Droszczyński, Bogusław Semotiuk, and Paweł Kruk playing the four parts. By that time, Grabowski had become Schaeffer's director. A year later, the second version was produced, in which Droszczyński and Semiotiuk were replaced by Janusz Peszek and Andrzej Kierc. In this second version, Grabowski – still a director – reduced the role of music and scenography, focusing more on acting and improvisation. The third version of *Quartet* under Grabowski's direction opened on September 15, 1981, in Teatr Polski (Polish Theatre) in Poznań. In this third version, the four players were portrayed by Jacek Chmielnik, Bogdan Słomiński, Janusz Łagodziński, and Janusz Peszek. This version relied even more heavily on the actors' skills of improvisation. Since its premiere, the *Quartet* has been so successful that it has been staged fifteen times, by practically every major Polish theatre. *Quartet* has also travelled extensively around the world, including to places such as Bogotá, Colombia. The play was filmed by Polish Television Theatre in 1991, under the direction of Mikolaj Grabowski.

The premise of the play is simple: four male actors dressed in tuxedos mime a music quartet. Likewise, the actor-musicians are balanced between theatre and concerto. In the program note to the original production of *Quartet*, Schaeffer wrote that he is not a playwright but a composer, interested in having his music performed by actors. As Ewa Kofin (1978) points out, the performance of music is a *performance* in itself, a ritual involving gestures, movements, and facial expressions. Having the actors enact them in *Quartet* draws attention to that kind of ritualistic, performative side of music, thus blending the distinctions between the two genres: music and acting. Thus, with *Quartet*, Schaeffer's Instrumental Theatre began to differ from that of Mauricio Kagel. For Schaeffer, the definition of music is broader than the traditional definition of sound made by musical instruments: Schaeffer's definition entails "action in and against the music," and "towards music." It entails

NON-music, ANTI-music, META-music, and TRANS-music. Such a broadened definition allows him to expand his artistic range without losing touch with music. NON-music is something else than music, poetry, painting, etc., but in relationship to music. Otherwise, it would function as music. ANTI-music goes against the established musical canons. META-music is something in between music and other phenomena, and TRANS-music is an art that can be treated as music. [...] Schaeffer's Instrumental Theatre is unique, as in his INTER-relations between different variants of music, the typical elements of Instrumental Theatre – instrumental acting and imaginary music (i.e., visual music) – disappear. What we get instead is a kind of metaphor of music, performance that's outside of fields and genre, one that can't be easily classified. (Kofin 1978: xx)

Miming the musical quartet, the actors make us aware of 'acting' as a process of miming: if musicians need to produce music, what, then, is the role of actors on stage? If their bodies are their instruments, what is it they produce? The movements of a musical quartet replace acts and scenes; the text – both musical and nonmusical – incorporates counterpoint (the relationship between two or more harmonically interdependent voices that are simultaneously independent in contour and rhythm), and aleatoricism, (the use of chance in the process of artmaking). The formula makes the play a closed work: there is nothing superfluous, and the ending is at the end.

The text is absurd and often contradictory, as if the actors don't hear or don't want to hear each other. They often argue with each other about trivial things, clown around, making absurd gestures and ridiculous acrobatic tricks, losing their focus and drifting away from the main action they're asked to perform. Each is enclosed in his own world, focused on himself. It is like a "quadruple monologue," as Schaeffer put it. The actors talk next to each other rather than to each other. The play is also a quartet of personalities: each character is different, and each has a different weakness: women, sports, alcohol, or gambling. Together, they create a particular polyphony. The twenty-five episodic scenes have neither plot as such, nor a dramatic structure in the Aristotelian sense. Written with almost mathematical precision, they include music scenes, dialogues, metatheatrical scenes, and visual scenes. Their geometry and structure is juxtaposed with the men's double-layered personalities. To quote Joanna Zajac (1998):

> The men have a strong sense of their own superiority and individuality, but they are average Joes with mediocre talents, and overblown ambitions. On the one hand, they appear to be sophisticated, but on the other, they drown in the everyday banality of their existence. They play boyish games, only to turn in the next second to adult aggression. They are obsessed with typically masculine preoccupations: football, vodka, gambling and hookers. Scene XVII focuses almost exclusively on typical male struggles. (129)

The play's elegant structure of a musical quartet enhances and delineates the male vulgarity. As Schaeffer puts it in the program notes to the first production:

> *Quartet for Four Actors* is a theatrical essay on music, men, their passion, their drive for fame, recognition, but also their fears. They are musicians, devoted to their work, but it's only appearance. The audience elegantly eliminates everything that reaches beyond their performance. They admire their passion, their teamwork, coordination of their movements, their seemingly perfect connection, without the conductor showing them what to do. [...] *Quartet* in music is a symbol of true pure perfection. But the musicians? Are they also pure? [...] I show their ambitions and their vices, their obsessions, triviality, proclivity for clichés, lack of intelligence, narrow landscape of dreams and desires.

The play mocks the artificiality of TV language and the pretenses of the artists, who are unable to communicate with each other. In the program notes to the 1982 version at the Słowacki Theatre in Cracow, the dramaturg, Marian Stala wrote that

> the author doesn't give his actor words that would carry some sense, but words that lose sense. He gives them a situation of lack. Their role is to transform it, take such a risk in front of the audience that would transform that negativity into positivity... Each time, the results are unpredictable.

In the program Schaeffer wrote that *Quartet for Four Actors* has

> elements of a morality play *à rebours* [in reverse]: the laughter
> it provokes, gives way to suspicion that who the author truly
> mocks is his audience (the spirit of Gogol seems to be watching
> over the show).

At the end of the show, all four of them freeze like a sculpture, mute and still as in the first scene. Schaeffer noted that in a musical quartet, the musicians practice to become one organism, but in *Quartet*, they fail, coming full circle to the same moment, still separate and alone in their delusory togetherness.

In 1992, Teatr Nowy (New Theatre) in Poznan staged an all-female version, *Quartet for Four Actresses*, under the direction of Julia Wernio. For this version, Schaeffer wrote two additional scenes: an overture and an intermezzo. The four parts were played by Grażyna Korin, Dorota Lulka, Daniela Popławska, and Maria Rybarczyk. The typical male problems have been replaced by women's chitchat – rendered more gender-specific by the use of period costumes. The staging was critically acclaimed, with many critics pointing out the humor of the production. One of them wrote that "Four actresses, Eves, play out with talent and aplomb the truths and stereotypes of being a woman, an actress. The line between triviality and nobility of an art disappears. They are forced to constantly pretend, put on new masks, new costumes" ("Scena Nowa" 1993). This gendered version of *Quartet* revealed the universality of Schaeffer's play, but also brought forth a new social dimension of his text. In 2009, a young performance group, Grupa Dochodzeniowa, staged a mixed gender version of *Quartet* under the direction of Beata Fudalej with Mateusz Ławrynowicz, Dorota Kuduk (guest), Jarosław Sacharski, and Agata Sasinowska.

Scenario for Three Actors (Scenariusz dla trzech aktorów) is a metatheatrical play about theatre and theatre artists: their private conflicts, antics, neuroses, desires, and artistic aspirations humorously deconstructed. Winner of many prestigious international awards, *Scenario* has been a permanent fixture in many Polish theatres since its premiere in 1987. Although it was written in 1970, it took seventeen years for the play to be performed for the first time. It opened at Theatre STU (Theatre of One Hundreds) in Cracow, with Mikolaj Grabowski (who also directed it), Andrzej Grabowski, and Jan Peszek. At the theatre festival in Szczecin, the production received seven awards, and in 1988 it was filmed by the Polish Television Theatre. *Scenario* has been staged in various versions in fourteen Polish theatres, and it continues to be shown at Theatre STU with the same cast to this day, a run of more than twenty years. It has been shown in Vienna, Budapest, Essen, and Berlin, among other cities. The core of the spectacle is a conversation between two actors and the director, or as some critics call it, a rehearsal. Most recently, Malgorzata Klimczak (2012) called the show "an intelligent conversation about art with the audience." Considering that Mikolaj Grabski was also the actual director of the show, the staging once again challenged the delicate line between fiction and reality. The metatheatrical situation traps the characters in stasis: like Beckett's Didi and Gogo, they are unable to move on because they're caught in an intellectual and emotional catch-22, dependent on each other's passions, paranoia, and antagonism. They strive for power and recognition, somewhat tragically aware that their position as artists is already fundamentally questionable. The line between reality and the absurd is once again blurred. The show brings forth familiar Schaefferian themes of the role of art and the fundamentally impossible position of the artist as both clown and priest. The show received critical acclaim, with critics particularly impressed by the humor of the production and the acting skills. In 2002, Teatr Syrena (Mermaid Theatre) in Warsaw staged an all-female version of the show under the direction of Bogusław Semotiuk, with Dorota Gorjanow, Anna Deka, and Iwona Chołuj. Like the all-male version, the production was an instant hit, and it was replayed in a number of other Polish theatres in the next decade.

Intrigued by Schaeffer's popularity and writing style, I began translating his plays in 2001. He sent me all of his plays and gave me full access to his manuscripts. Since then, we have maintained an active correspondence. Schaeffer graciously appreciates that I was able to capture the poetic, musical, and playful quality of his writing. Most of all, however, he likes that I "get" his peculiar sense of humor, since, as Virginia Woolf famously noted, "humour is the first of the gifts to perish in a foreign tongue." The translator's task with Schaeffer's plays is complex. First, one must understand the script's elaborate word games and puns. The plays are full of such linguistic gems as anacoluthons (rhetorical trick of changing syntax within the same sentence), solecisms (purposeful and playful grammatical mistakes), and intentional catachreses (misappropriation of words and sentences). These rhetorical devices are enough to give a translator a headache. But in addition to mastering the plays' sociological, cultural, and linguistic context, one must capture their intricate musical structure: the rhythm and tonality of language. Finally, the translator must address the text's visual arrangement: here, words are like notes; their order and page placement must be preserved. You don't just translate; like Schaeffer, you must compose the play.

More recently, Schaeffer has become known in international theatre and music circles for multimedia performances that include both his musical compositions and his dramatic texts. The most famous production is *Schaeffer's Era*, an interactive audiovisual, multimedia performance that reflects Schaeffer's own musings on contemporary culture, the art of composition, and its perception. The show was created in 2009 by the Aurea Porta Foundation to celebrate Schaeffer's 80th birthday. This brilliant multimedia improv gala features the Polish National Radio Orchestra conducted by Agnieszka Duczmal, the Olga Szwajgier Jazz Quartet, Bogusław Schaeffer on piano, soloist Urszula Dudziak, Schaeffer's instrumental actors such as Marek Frackowiak, Witold Obloza, and Agnieszka Wielgosz, and Schaeffer's play *A Multimedia Thing*. In 2010, an ambitious two-hour work was staged at the EICC as part of the Edinburgh Festival. Professor Richard Demarco, the festival's co-founder, said he had "not seen anything like it since the times of Kantor," calling Schaeffer's piece "one of the best productions since the festival was launched several dozen years ago." Both the *Edinburgh Spotlight* and the *Herald Scotland* awarded it 4 of 5 stars, calling it a "tremendous show in honour of an original talent." The *Edinburgh Spotlight* wrote that "*Schaeffer's Era* provides a rare and brief opportunity to be immersed in a compelling multisensory vision of a unique individual." *Schaeffer's Era* breaks down the barriers between a variety of genres, providing a bold vision of a true Renaissance man. The success of the original production prompted Aurea Porta to mount the next version in 2012.

WORKS CITED

Benjamin, Walter. 1988. "The work of art in the age of mechanical reproduction". 1935. Reprinted in *Illuminations,* trans. Harry Zohn. Random House: New York.

Caprioli, Albert. 1999. "Bogusław Schaeffer, der unsichtbare Klassiker der Musik" [Bogusław Schaeffer: The invisible classicist of the music]. In Sugiera and Zając, *Bogusław Schaeffer: Composer and playwright,* 103–17.

Cooper, Neil. "Era Schaeffera, Edinburgh International Conference Centre." *Herald Scotland* [Glasgow] 23 Aug. 2010: n. pag. *Herald Scotland.* Newsquest, 23 Aug. 2010. Web. <http://www.heraldscotland.com/arts-ents/stage-visual-arts/era-schaeffera-edinburgh-international-conference-centre-1.1049794>.

Cooper, Neil. "The 13-day Week of a Musical Genius." *Herald Scotland.* Newsquest, 20 Aug. 2010. Web. <http://www.heraldscotland.com/arts-ents/stage-visual-arts/the-13-day-week-of-a-musical-genius-1.1049325>.

JOC. 2011. "Ten rewelacyjny Peszek" [Phenomenal Peszek]. *Dziennik Polski,* December 1. Polish Theatre Portal, <http://www.e-teatr.pl/pl/artykuly/129169.html>.

"FRINGE REVIEW – Era Schaeffera (Venue 150 / Universal Arts)." *Edinburgh Spotlight.* N.p., 21 Aug. 2010. Web. <http://www.edinburghspotlight.com/2010/08/fringe-review-era-schaeffera-venue-150-universal-arts/>.

Karasińska, Marta. 1999. "Dialog, non-dialog of Bogusław Schaeffer". In Sugiera and Zając, *Bogusław Schaeffer: Composer and playwright,* 45–70.

Klimczak, Małgorzata. 2012. "Błyskotliwa dyskusja z publicznością o sztuce" [Witty Conversation With Audience About Art]. *Głos Szczeciński* 51/01.03.12 (March 9). Polish Theatre Portal, <http://www.e-teatr.pl/pl/artykuly/134334.html>.

Kofin, Ewa. 1978. "Teatr Instrumentalny" [Instrumental Theatre] *Scena,* 6. Reprinted in program notes to production at the Teatr Polski [Polish Theatre] in Poznań, 1981.

Lichocka, Sylwia. 2010. "Aktorstwo możliwe" [The Possible Acting]. *Informator Festiwalowy,* 1/27.11 (November 28). Polish Theatre Portal, <http://www.e-teatr.pl/pl/artykuly/106890.html>.

Oakes, Guy. 1980. "The theory of interpretation". In *Essays on interpretation in social science,* by Georg Simmel. Manchester: Manchester University Press. 57–86.

Peszek, Jan. 1999. Moj mistrz: Schaeffer [My Maestro: Schaeffer]. In Sugiera and Zając, *Bogusław Schaeffer: Composer and playwright,* 177–92.

Piotrowska, Ewa. 1992. "Kwartet jakiego nie było" [Quartet As Never Seen Before]. *Głos Wielkopolski,* 122 (May 25). Polish Theatre Portal, <http://www.e-teatr.pl/pl/artykuly/130942.html>.

Pulka, Leszek. 2003. *Gazeta Wyborcza*, February 19. Quoted on Evoé Performing Artists website (accessed on Dec. 14, 2008).

Scena Nowa. 1993. *Gazeta Wielkopolska,* 49 (February 27). Polish Theatre Portal, <http://www.e-teatr.pl/pl/artykuly/130952.html>.

Stabro, Stanisław. 2003. *Literatura Polska 1944–2000, w zarysie.* Cracow: Wydawnictwo Uniwersytetu Jagiellonskiego.

Sugiera, Małgorzata, and Joanna Zając, eds. 1999. *Bogusław Schaeffer: Composer and playwright.* Kraków: Księgarnia Akademicka.

Tytkowska, Agata. 1999. "Dramaturgia Bogusława Schaeffera" [The Dramaturgy of Bogusław Schaeffer]. In Sugiera and Zając, *Bogusław Schaeffer: Composer and playwright.* Kraków: Księgarnia Akademicka. 157-175.

Wolff, Kurt H., ed. and trans. 1964. Introduction to *The Sociology of Georg Simmel,* by Georg Simmel. New York: Free Press. xvii–lxiii.

Zając, Joanna. 1998. *Dramaturgia Schaeffera* [The dramaturgy of Bogusław Schaeffer]. Salzburg, Austria: Collsch Edition.

Zając, Joanna. 1999. "Multimedialność w czasach niepewności" [Multimedia in Precarious Times]. In Sugiera and Zając, *Bogusław Schaeffer: Composer and playwright,* 11–26.

Žižek, Slavoj, 1989. *The sublime object of ideology.* Verso: London.

SCENARIO FOR A NON-EXISTING,
BUT POSSIBLE INSTRUMENTAL ACTOR

Jan Peszek, in *Scenario for a Non-Existing, but Possible Instrumental Actor*. Photo by Paweł Topolski, 10 November, 2009. Courtesy of Tarnowski Teatr im Ludwika Solskiego (Ludwig Solski Theatre, Tarnów)

SCENE ONE

Lights dimmed.
One single stream of lighting focused on the Actor, who is sitting at the table.
On the table – a lamp and a glass of water.

The Actor, staring at the audience, sits motionless.

...calm, focused, serious – nothing indicates what is about to happen...

The Actor starts speaking (calmly):

> The longer I'm involved in artmaking, the more clearly I see how dependent it is on external factors. What's more, the external factors always triumph, even when we're dealing with the most permanent, most established rules – rules that you'd think nothing could alter. As long as I'm "on my own," that is, as long as I'm in a relationship with my art only, concerned with its well-being only – working for its own sake – then, everything is all right: everything is the way it is; I know what is what. Value judgments, work ethics, inspirations, intentions, and even aspirations – everything is arranged according to some spiritual "plan" that fits ideally into what you do. If this internal harmony were to disappear, art would become impossible, or at least, it would suffer its own "impossibility."

(Reading.)

> When the artwork emerges from the inside to the "outside," nothing is as it's supposed to be. It's as if we left a small child on the street and ordered it to "take care of himself." All right, most likely some good people will take care of the child, and eventually, he'll find his way home, but that's not how it is with a work of art. A work of art will wander the streets of the world, understanding neither the world nor how it got there, and it will be awfully lonely.

He gets up, leaves, returns...

Sits motionless for a while.

He peels an apple (25 seconds).

Grows poetically pensive and starts speaking, while chewing on the apple. He's speaking in contrast to his poetic daydreaming. He begins intimately, in the tone of a servant; then, as if confessing, finally, at the end, he finishes in a matter-of-fact tone of voice.

I've held quiet for a long time, but now, since we're constantly talking about it anyways, how art is understood differently than we, the artists, understand it, I can finally say it: more and more often art lives off charity; most artists – perhaps even without realizing it – are beggars. Only thanks to the exquisite gullibility of the youngest of them, society still experiences that drive, that passion for art – that goes against the commonsense notion that – if one's to be a "material man" – one should find more practical occupation. Personally, I believe that art is only for those who couldn't otherwise live without it, who would devote themselves to it regardless...for sure, and unconditionally...

(From memory:)

Those who have already experienced some success can't bear what it does to them; art makes one hungry. After a while, even success appears insufficient, unsatisfying. Everyone knows that, everyone except perhaps some dull dupes. Every day, we encounter a lie called self-promotion. That lie is necessary – not just to make us feel better about ourselves, to keep us in a kind of spiritual equilibrium – but also in order to "hold on" to what we've already accomplished. If a singer were to say that he had a horrible performance at La Scala last night, nobody would ever talk to him again. Let me point it out that society, indeed, forces the artist to lie. I'm citing a drastic example here because it best illustrates many other social problems. We have in art the so-called sphere of reality, in which everything happens the way it really is; *(He begins laughing, increasingly inappropriately...)* (violinist X gave a concert in Barcelona, compositor Y wrote a

piece, a philharmonic concert took place in city Z, etc.);
and the sphere of imagination, which generally depends
on the artist's aspirations and intentions, and of course,
on the institutions (every piece composed by composer
R provokes great interest; each tournée of group S was
a great success owed to its brilliant conductor and its
musicians, etc. etc.). Let's think about it for a moment,
who informs us and how about these real facts and the
imaginary ones (yes, let us use that word in this context).
We are informed of them by the same sources and…in
the same manner, even though both of these spheres have
nothing to do with each other. It seems that in modern
art what's most important is clouding the big picture:
perhaps that's why art criticism gives way to news, and
news gives way to delusions. It happens also because
in our times, art is grossly multiplied, eclipsing wider
and wider social circles, losing at the same time its own
autonomy – the kind it used to have when it was still
saying something. The simple fact that reproductions are
available to everyone (once one used to play the piano,
now one plays on the radio) tells us a lot about where we
are.

(Calmly:)

Another classic example: in the past, performances were
often premieres, and now, all we do are replications,
re-interpretations of old things, or very old things. Pra-
premieres are a true rarity these days. Strange thing
happened: we still do music, but we no longer do it as an
art.

*(Longer preparation for open composition; fixing of the props;
exactly, putting them all in one place / farther away from the table)*

OPEN COMPOSITION

(Each activity is accompanied by a different acoustic sound.)

Activities: pounding the chair on the floor, wailing, dancing, eating and drinking (with burping), yelling at the wall, crying, calling, hitting the table with wet rag, singing, dragging some things behind, laughing, limping, hitting a strung fishing line with a wet cloth, riding a bike across the stage, screaming horrified, playing harmonica under a sheet – long notes, deep breathing, changing clothes, screaming horrified, blinding the audience with a reflector, fury and gentility intertwined illustrated with words and gestures.

(In absolute exhaustion, the actor returns to his main text; reading, horribly "sipping" – speaking incompetently, gradually...false accents.)

I've said before that the image of modern art is blurry, unclear. Interesting fact though: today's artist when asked why he does what he does, wouldn't be able to answer.

Most certainly, the profession of an artist treated strictly professionally should be questioned. First of all, the profession of an artist-creator, unlike artist-recreator, or creator we could call – not quite nicely but appropriately – reproducer, shouldn't be even considered in these divagations. This kind of profession *(Pauses...e...e...etc.)* will survive as long as there is the will to reproduce art. Let us note that the artists from the East customarily recreate centuries-old traditions; it is possible that in the future, that is all we'll be doing, recreating art, diverting it; what we're experiencing today is without a doubt a symptom of such a possibility.

(...the Actor shows horrible exhaustion with this one gesture... maybe: sweat – too much – taking off his shirt – horrible moans – like a mine worker, dead and hollow; sits down by the appropriate table, continues calmly, pragmatically:)

Contemporary music is sentenced to autoreproduction. It multiplies and reproduces all by itself, since recorded, it is no longer one unique piece of work, but is destined for mass reproduction and mass redistribution. Let us notice that by reproducing and redistributing art we devalue it in two ways: for one, by the fact that it no longer reaches the appropriate audience, and two, by the fact that we devoid it of its original aura, the aura from which it was originally conceived (the composer's idea, the set of expressive tools which he considered his own, authentic and possible "to use"). On reproductions, someone always makes money, and it is not an art that benefits the most, that's for sure. Art is only concerned with its own perfection. And here, Ladies and Gents, we're approaching a point that deserves our closer scrutiny.

Let's think for a minute what role an artist had in the era in which his image was completely different, in Romanticism, of course. We're talking, obviously, about an artist-art-maker, not a re-maker.

In the Romantic period, the artist drew attention to himself, using various archaic tricks, in the same way that a magician, prophet, mystic, or holy man would. The less he was needed in public life – and let us remember that this was an era of tyrants, autocratic rulers, aristocrats and bankers – the more he "scuffled" his way through their vestiges of power, trumpeting the possible goods he could bring into the public debate, making himself into someone indispensable. Now, of course, we see that it was all a deception, perhaps springing from the oversaturation with daydreams and easy (but always false) identification with a Platonic ideal; perhaps what motivated his aspirations was a desire to find oneself amongst the better "society" (perhaps that is why the artists of today still reserve the most contempt for other artists the way that butlers harbor visible contempt for their "fellow" servants). Perhaps – and here, some psychoanalysis might be helpful – the artist wanted to avenge himself for all the humiliations that he experienced on an everyday basis (let us recall Joseph Haydn, for example, who not only customarily wore livery, but often performed his quartets behind "closed doors" to the accompaniment of loud conversations). In the end, it doesn't matter what motivated all these delusionary artistic usurpations; the fact is that the artists succeeded at convincing their society that they were indispensable, with their mission and all. This époque is long gone, but all the delusions are still with us, the foul odor of pretense without merit, since, as we made it clear, the role of the artist went downhill.

SCENE TWO – THE ACTOR'S MONOLOGUE

I imagine today's artist in a brand-new light: he's a man
focused on his own work, a self-contained man living
in his inner world. He reveals only a fraction of who
he really is to the outside world, primarily through his
aesthetics, pedagogically or perhaps culturally framed.
He is indifferent, at first, to the popularity of his work;
he knows the current market well enough not to have
any illusions. He knows that even the slightest touch of
commercialism can stifle all of his creativity.

(Looking at the audience, as if he has an eye on someone.)

You know what? When you're staring at me so insistently,
I can't act. I can't concentrate. When you're in a theatre,
you should look attentively – but discreetly. *(Pause.)*
Discretion... Do you even know what discretion is? I see
someone shoplifting at the supermarket, but I pretend I
don't see it. Discretion! I see him steal, but I say nothing.
What am I supposed to say? 'Oh, I see that today you're
working in high-end perfumes. Yesterday, I saw you in
the households aisle, by the shelf with the toilet paper.
But you can't steal anything from there, oh, no, because
the sons of bitches wrap the damn toiled paper in such
huge bags that they're impossible to hide. But here,
you casually throw a few bottles of perfume, worth
the equivalent of some poor clerk's paycheck, into an
open briefcase, and voilà.' But I don't tell him that, no.
Discretion. If I see him tomorrow, I might wink at him. I
might even greet him...discreetly.

To fully grasp the modern artist, one must – alas – one
must turn to modern philosophy. Modern man lives in
a world that determines his actions so completely that
all he's got left is just the tiniest margin of freedom.
Regardless of where and how he lives, he never makes
decisions about himself autonomously. And, on the other
hand, decisions that are being made are never about him.

(Speaking.)

Modern man suffers for his lack of opportunities for self-crystallization. As a solid object, he emits most of his spiritual substance, unable to hold onto it. He can momentarily retain some of his 'qualities' – but only for as long as he can hold onto a trump card that someone else will soon mix into the deck according to the rules of the game.

He starts sawing the wood, nailing wooden boards to each other, or he does something else, some kind of physical action for a longer period of time. As he is working, he interacts with the audience: 'Can you hold it here? Come on, put some muscle into it!... You obviously never do any physical labor. OK, yeah, that's better. Just like that... calmly, relaxed..." He repeats:

Modern man suffers for his lack of opportunities for self-crystallization. As a solid object, he emits most of his spiritual substance, unable to hold on to it.

(Disdainful, arrogant...)

Although modern man occasionally happens to be an actor (generally, in some unfortunate public spectacle – after all, a single day of fame is a fate reserved for criminals and victims) – modern man, most of the time, is an actor who grows more passive with each passing day. Still, he can't be accused of callous indifference. The world, after all, is indifferent towards him, and man is always a product of his world. What's important to him is a matter of complete indifference to everyone else (nowadays it seems that's how they like to explain the shortages of decent heroes in modern novels; modern heroes are always just slightly inferior to Leopold Bloom). To repeat: the modern artist has lost his once-privileged position and become "just a man in the crowd." And when a man in the crowd calls something out, we don't call him an "artist"–we call him a "spokesperson." No one says "that was Great Man X calling out!" because the spokesperson's voice is drowned in a sea of other more-or-less mysterious voices (either negating or confirming the popular transcribed speeches).

And thus, we come to the main que. . . . [*He cuts it off abruptly at "que" and waits for someone to take pity on him and finish "stion"*] and let's remember that this question has always been important: how can the modern artist draw attention to himself? We hear more and more often that the artist must (indeed, *must*) find for himself some kind of role, because simply making art is no longer enough. It can be any role: the role of defender of the tradition, the role of politically engaged artist, the role of "popular" or "renowned" artist, the role of avant-garde genius, and so on. Once he's assumed a role, the artist must stay in character, just like clowns stay in character for their skits. French writers of past generations taught us that roles can be cast off like gloves (there is something pathetic in this ability, it's a kind of human moral deficiency). But the possibility of constantly changing one's roles doesn't necessarily mean that one always has the ability to do so, as simply being an artist often takes so much effort that negotiations with the world are left unattended. The modern artist is a man who chooses his own fate – within the limits of his individual possibilities and abilities – but if he wants to accomplish anything, he must remain faithful to himself. Reading biographies of the great masters, we learn that their individual fates – despite all the pleasure and satisfaction the world has derived from their work – their individual fates were often horrifyingly inhuman: proof positive that the world always mocks its chosen ones.

(Blending in with the text.)

A 150-year-old Hadji

who made the pilgrimage to Mecca a second time,

not remembering that

a hundred years ago

he'd already made the pilgrimage,

was given a transistor radio by sailors who took pity on him.

He's got to live one hundred and fifty years

just to

listen in his old age

to a small box spewing

    rashly composed tunes

    and fake news.

        A long day

           has been growing inside you like a spear

           piercing your natural rhythm and

           perpetual state of being,

    time turns into small particles

    filled with mumbling actions

    that have no meaning,

    and nonsense pulsations of

    a neurotically alive matter,

    life

– filled with the void of inane habits,

    which ought to say something about a man

        but end up saying something only

        about his knee-jerk reactions.

Tearing words from the empty newspaper

    tasty distasteful bites

    he swallows them on the sly

    with soup poured into the bowl of dreams,

feeding in this way his second self,

his inner hunger artist

the missing spirit

who not so long ago

didn't want to gorge on just anything

who was searching in everything

for something for himself

unsatisfied

with the collectively-fed imagination

who was afraid of matter

afraid of crude behavior

afraid of his own downfall

Drinking the urine liquid

of daily news and entertainment gossips

that are neither new nor entertaining

opening his mouth like a child

waiting for milk

that turned into a poison

– stuffing his benighted pockets

with everything

that's expendable and cruel,

as he runs away from his own cruelty

compensating for his weakness

by sharing his ill imagination with those who urgently

like him

need money.

Coming back to their homes

    Filled with empty chatter

hitting their heads on too low an entrance to reality

    which they don't understand,

they take off the masks of their other polite nature

content to wash their hands of the common dirt,

    that they brushed against

    unaware of having done so,

sitting at life's late supper,

    which

in no way resembles the suppers they used to eat,

loosening the belt on their spirit

    the belt by which they were led their entire lives

vomiting up the distaste at

the day's pleasure derived from

    social interaction with others.

Pale light falls on the work table,

there is nothing on it that

couldn't have been swept aside with a brush of the hand,

one feels exhausted

enlivened only by the worries

and meaningless problems of others.

    Long days

    have been growing inside you like a . . .

    (– halt!)

(Continuing the lecture.)

The modern artist pays a steep price for the delusions of his predecessors: the past world cannot be evoked, even for art's sake. All that's left is the present world, and the present world mercilessly insists he meet its demands. Today, even the greatest artist must "keep to himself" his demands on the world. If he manifests his hunger, if he shows his dissatisfaction with the world's preconditions, he loses. There is always, of course, the possibility of surrendering to outside pressures to save oneself. But from the endless whitewashing of one's talents one emerges only seemingly clean. In truth, all this writhing leaves a permanent mark; one becomes a caricature of an artist. The loud complaints of all these well-to-do masochists are by now familiar. They dream of the epic heroism of someone devoted solely to his art, but they never realize these dreams.

(From another place.) What is a genius without fame – He once asked – but then, another question occurred to him: what can fame do even to the greatest genius? Why do people so impatiently and doggedly strive for fame? Isn't its value manufactured and fundamentally useless? Inconsequential, senseless things gain wild acclaim for no reason. Is it really that important who the fastest runner in the 100-yard dash is, if that doubtful privileged first place usually lasts for barely a few minutes? (it did happen). A Hindu guru was once asked why he's not interested in sports. He replied that he knows that someone will be first, and he's not interested in who will that be. We all bend under pressure, doing something we don't want to do, caring about something we really don't care about, remembering details no more important than a list of names in a phone book from fifty years ago. As a result, we know a lot, while truly knowing so little that when compared to our grandparents we come out looking like complete fools.

He wasn't meandering; his thinking was directional, that's for sure. He believed that there are three kinds of thinking: circular thinking, which is based on one theme only, wrapped up in high-minded, but utterly pointless pseudo-intellectual babble; layered thinking (the kind that we find in the writing of that guy Heidegger), which compels us with the logic of its thought, devised for no other purpose but to shame us into submission, flustering us that such deep thought has never occurred to us; and finally, the third kind, directional thinking, which connects various ideas into a seemingly disjointed system that nonetheless occasionally makes sense.

Fame, manufactured values, runner, our pseudo-interests, phone book, grandparents, stupefied with the future – He was pondering quite seriously all these things, whether or not it would be possible to recreate artificially such a stream of thoughts, so that one could then find some thinking patterns for them, for example – monotony – sadness – genitals – abstract painting – vaccinations. He even began creating quite impressive configuration himself when suddenly someone riding on the steps of an opened bus fell out of it – thus ruining the above-mentioned configuration at its most intriguing moment. The bus went on its way – who was that man? What was the most important thing about him? Not his name, that's for certain. His profession, perhaps? (if he's without one, what then?). Or maybe he was simply a man who fell out of the bus (the bus was turning the corner really slowly, so the man, fortunately, escaped without a scratch). He thought that for many people, the man could be just "a man who fell out of the bus," and nothing more than that. But should this be so? Is that right? A few centuries ago, a man with a halberd guarding the gates of the castle could not be identified; he was anonymous just like a local medieval grocer or wandering preacher. Today, a physicist falls out of the bus and all we can think of is the law of physics – the centrifugal force – that threw him out (that's a scandal: a physicist and he allows himself to be thrown out of the bus by his own law – reality has its own sense of humor).

He got out of the bus – stumbling and stumbled upon – he looked at his watch, which for years has been running a few minutes early and which serves – for sophisticated people like him – only as a convenient eye-catcher; after all, the aesthetics of the jam-packed bus had to be counterbalanced somehow); he crossed a busy street and stepped onto the nearby sidewalk – this neighborhood's only accomplishment (on the newly remodeled sidewalk one could freely get lost in one's thoughts without worrying about approaching buses or trams with functional brakes certainly, but often driven by people without them). The shortage of proteins, fats, sugars, vitamins, water and whatnot – that is to say, the hunger – began bothering him. Most people don't devote even five minutes a week to keeping their minds in a constant state of readiness, but to keep their metabolism running smoothly they don't hesitate to venture into the most malodorous joints, wasting there a quite substantial part of their lives. That's how life is: unappetizing, but dependent on our appetites.

(He freezes.)

SCENE THREE

Suddenly:

Pantomime: 'Charles' walks slowly, pees, turns around, pees, etc....

...as if zipping his pants...

(From memory.)

> Let's get back to where we started. It is certain that in the modern world, we no longer have that cultural dividing line that separates what's noble from what's beneath good taste, what's good from what's bad, what's truly artistic from what's common.

(From memory.)

> One time, I'm walking with Charlie – we're just walking and talking, no big deal – but suddenly Charlie's got to go. We went on the side – a few trees here and there – Charlie begins to take a piss. In the mid-dle *(He looks at someone and stops in the middle.)*...

(From memory.)

> What we're lacking today (lacking, really? perhaps not so much, if we were lacking it, we would have done something about it...), what we're lacking is a social code that would nurture, cultivate the artistic, the aesthetic consciousness.

> ...such little ol' trees – Charlie's standin' and pissin.' In the middle of it, a chick comes by, a young, good-looking one *(Continuing, without breaking eye contact with the group of audience members he has chosen beforehand, he speaks the main text – which can be read.)*

> Just like during the last century it was delusional to see every artistic act as a messianic vision, today, it is equally delusional to ascribe value to every art object (paintings are a particularly good example of that strange mismatch).

... jde divka, takova mlada sleczna a velmi zajimava. Karl – povida – to nejde tak, čeba aspoń konczit, to vubec neni fajn... .

(Speaking in Czech, he mixes up some sociological theories, gets tongue-tied and – finally – returns to the main text.)

Chtěl jsem řikat něco užitečneho všichnim skladatelum a vědcum. Kritéria tykajícíse současně hudby...

(Continuing.)

We can't even dream about modern style because style emerges only in conditions where such a social code exists. We're destined not just to descend into chaos (as some experts predict), but also into a complete devaluation of a value.

The more art imitates life...the more vulgar are the art objects.

(Suddenly.)

"Charlie – for Pete's sake – hurry up – I say – a woman's coming our way." And he's back at me:

"Pete, what are you fretting about, there are two billion and two hundred thousand women out there, and she's one of them" *(Halts abruptly.)*

Art requires refinement, unconditional devotion, and all such qualities. Even Kant, the most austere of all thinkers, considered them necessary and essential for art. In place of these qualities, we now have different ones creeping into our lives: starting with the more innocuous ones such as popularity and easiness, and ending (oh, when will we finally stop being offended!) on the recently quite popular one like 'selling out' (a simple solution would be to conflate the value with the price; real art – that's what it teaches us – has no price; it is priceless).

> Es gibt – sagte Karlheinz – insgesamt zwo Milliardem zwohundert und siebenudfufziś Tausend Weiber in der Welt, und hier geht es um eine einzige Person, eine Hure vielleicht.

(With Lviv accent.)

Contemporary works of art have no address, hence they can move around, being bought and sold not according to their individual destinies, but like other commodities, etc. We increasingly sense it that art is a product of the past; its value is measured by the passage of time. Even the greatest contemporary work of art can't measure up against a common vulgar clay bowl dug up from some ancient ruins. The artists of today try to create some kind of esoteric value, aura of time, around their work, as real art-making takes a long, long time. What modern art does have plenty of are art experts with highly sublimated tastes.

(Nearly in the same tone.)

> Women – he says – there are two billion of them, and this is just one nice girl. – Well, maybe not too nice, just look at her ass hanging out like that... see, bro, nothing to worry about, it's just a common ho...

(Nearly in the same tone.)

The era of selfless expertise is long gone. Today's art experts gladly sell their services – like commercial artists – to the cause of the homogenized, devoid-of-meaning "reception" of artwork (the question "who'll buy it" trumps – evil triumphs, cackling with delight – the question "in which way is this good"). *(Suddenly normal.)* The pathological rifts of yesteryear ("nothing bordering on something") are the norm in modern art. The modern world absorbs automatically, out of habit, all kinds of artworks, from masterworks of great inspiration to various artistic jokes (this is particularly true for visual art, perhaps because it is the most dis-autonomous and the least expressive of all arts; literature speaks of something, music says something, visual art has always been stuck in between these two worlds).

(Narrator, 1/4 intelligent and pretentious.)

The woman has left and I, saddened by the incident, begin to ponder the modern escalation and intensification of common boorishness (here!). Charlie doesn't know he is immoral – he assumes – perhaps maybe even likely rightly – that every woman is a 'ho,' and his physiological needs always take precedence over the less important issues of vulgar bourgeois morality.

We are at the crossroads, yes, us – that is why we must talk about it (one brief digression: a generation of artists that doesn't ponder art's *raison d'être* is a generation, that's for sure, but certainly, not of artists; the modern artist must be perfectly aware of the conditions in which he must live and create; it's difficult to be yourself; only a madman can fully be himself, the irony being that then, the poor madman, of course, isn't being himself; an artist is subject to the same antinomy, and his unwillingness to comprehend anything can be ascribed only to his pettiness).

(He sings – in tenor ang. from oratorio.)

Haj Czarlz ju aː e kle-wer boy. Aj ed-ma-a-a---ir you!

Hi Charles, you are a cle-ver boy. I ad-miiiii-re you!

(He repeats it twice, returning to the word "I" and continues right away "I – the question is...")

The question is to what degree modern artists are responsible for the current state of affairs. Careful listeners have most likely noticed by now that our contemplations revolve around ethics. One doesn't need to be worldly and sophisticated to know that art dealers are not somehow released – due to the dishonest nature of their profession – from all ethical considerations. Why dishonest, you'll ask? If you are even just a little familiar with how the market works, you know that everything, I mean everything, except true honesty, works well in it. It is sufficient that only one art dealer from a competing firm lowers his ethical standards just a little bit for you to quickly fall off the market bandwagon. Art dealers can be justified in their dishonesty only insofar as the value of artworks can be fluid; errors are made consistently and one never truly knows how much things are worth. In such circumstances, the artist is the only one who can be ethical if he feels like it, if it's worth anything to him.

It's quite apparent that ethical standards by themselves act in a creative manner: let me remind you that art "creates" an artist, teaching him about ethical values, since in the very first stage of art-making that act itself is always pure, selfless, ethical and beautiful. Not being in control of his own life, the modern artist succumbs to external pressures (here, we can consider the word 'dealer' in its broader context, from art dealer to other dealers in other social contexts); he succumbs often quite willingly, as temptations are many (*être et avoir* – to be and to have – a constant dilemma of modern philosophy).

> Charles – *tu est un grand virtuose des acte*: a true virtuoso, I added in French – an intellectual, yet one who's also not a stranger to an animalistic candor. That's what I value in you the most.

(Moving with the text towards his audience.)

(In front of the audience.)

Our world as of now is still under the sway of its institutions; it doesn't want to consider any new emerging components, being quite comfortable not thinking about them at all. Avoiding any discussions, our institutionalized world pretends that everything is the way it used to be, nothing ever changed, thus not realizing that new economic forces mess up the old order. This paradox creates more antinomies further complicating the big picture – everything changes really fast and even deeper symptoms of our culture are impermanent.

(He stops and asks, as if interrogating someone...)

Last name. . . .

Despite all that, we can draw some conclusions that would make it easier for us to understand our world. Here, I mean all the marginal art trends that appear spontaneously, gaining some traction before being completely absorbed by the very reality which they initially opposed.

When and in what circumstances did you last see Mr. Kowalski?

Such absorption is quite natural for art, even while the very appearance of the trends and processes is quite authentic. Let's note that even such popular musical trends like jazz, beat or pop barged into our lives without any questions, preparations or warnings.

Did he give you any money? – promise you something?

Of course, we can trace the genesis of these trends in the context of their own traditions, as well as "explain" them as forms of reaction and protest against the dominant culture, etc. etc. – but both of these analyses won't answer the pivotal question: why at "that particular time" these trends appeared, irritating everyone with their insolent supremacy.

Madame, your name? First and last...

In contemporary visual arts – which, for music, can be a model of actions and reactions, transformations and surprises – the changes we're speaking about are quite common.

Why are they quite common? Can you explain it?

In music, we are used to the necessity of solidifying everything that happens while never being quite sure how it will turn out (in visual arts, the speed of changes is at least certain). We never know what it is that we are dealing with.

(To another woman in the audience.) Maybe you know what we're dealing with here?

So, diagnosing a situation – in music – is always difficult: this difficulty is magnified by the fact that music is an auditory art where assimilation is much more difficult than it is in visual arts. In visual arts, our eye quickly accepts changing circumstances (I have to admit, this is a generalization, as even in visual arts, there are always exceptions where the artist uses uber-visual strategies to represent his ideas). Understanding and influencing musical processes is made difficult by the fact that the entire content of music lies outside of its material form (indeed, musical form is necessary only insofar as to carry other uber-material ideals; music is composed not for sounds, but for the multiplicity of relations which they evoke: every musical master who has ever advanced the field further than the average mass of sound makers has known that). Finally, not everything that's important for music can be understood for the simple reason that we're dealing here with components that establish a direct relationship between art-making, art being and art consuming. Most important in this equation is the discrepancy in reception of music between its author and its consumer. There are examples of a complete dissonance between these two poles of reception. A composer today can work in a sphere that is completely inaccessible for the consumer. It is true that there is absolutely nothing to understand in music (music is music, that's it); however, there can be discrepancies in reception of the idea behind the music.

> You know, Charlie, when you were standing there, so focused but also so relaxed, it came to me that you weren't just relieving yourself. It wasn't just about a simple physiological need. It was a protest against thoughtlessness and the base utilitarianism of the contemporary commercialized world. With your act – I go on, flattering him shamelessly – you showed everyone that you are a free man. Free not just from the social conventions and prejudices, but in the higher, spiritual sense. Don't fuck with me – Charlie cut me off, and he was right because carried away by my own eloquence I'd reach higher and higher, and who the hell knows what for.

(Bright light; the actor jumps on the table, and pulls the chair – throne – up on top of it.)

I, the King of Monaco, Munich and Monaster, encourage my people to listen to electronic music composed by my favorite court composer. Maestro, roll the tape!!!

(Loud, abrasive music; the actor screams over it, barely heard.) Beautiful music, isn't it? Graceful, even if it's electronic. *(He rocks idiotically to the rhythm of the music; after a while, he stops and freezes.)* I don't like this music. I don't like it. *(Pause.)* It's too quiet and too sad. Away with this music! *(Comes down from the table and takes down the chair.)* It's too bad I got rid of the inquisition in my country. I could torture and burn the damn composer on the big pyre together with his idiotic partitures. After a little

persuasion, he'd start writing gentler music, more suitable for my court and my poor subjects. *(Blackout; the Actor gets up on the table, lies down and moans, but audibly.)* Ah, ah… *(Pause.)* This Jung, this Jung, this idiot Jung. *(Falls asleep tired.)*

(Soft, pleasant music; in the darkness, the Actor stands up the table, looks down on the floor and then, on the audience.)

Nobody will deny that I, Freud, or more precisely, Professor Sigmund Freud, know psychology. But I am not interested in the psychology of crowds or even the psychology of the theatre audience. They can exist or not in whatever way they want. I'm interested in the psychology of the individual, like, for example, that darn Jung, who twists everything I ever said or wrote. That son of a bitch has it coming! *(Speaking directly to one chosen person in the audience.)* And you, why are you staring at me like that? You've never seen a psychologist? Why don't you drop by my office tomorrow at four. You'll lie down on the couch, tell me everything about yourself and I'll tell you how to properly behave in the theatre… For me, there are no difficult cases. Well, there was one, but I took care of it. *(Laughing.)* A guy went to college and became a psychologist, not a very good one, like Jung, or maybe even worse than that. So, that guy came up with the idea of how to treat the psychological issues of the psychologist. Medice, cura te ipsum.

And what a wise Epictetus said? Bear and forebear! Sustine et abstine! And what did the immortal Dante say? "Let them scratch wherever it itches." Paradiso, Canto XVII, apartment 129, sorry, line 129. *(To a chosen person from the audience.)* Do you know you can't smoke here? *(Expected protest in the audience.)* I know you don't smoke, even though you really want to; it's very easy to tell, just looking at your smelly yellowed fingers. *(Pause.)* I just wanted to make sure you know. You nod, that's good. One should always nod in response to the wise man. It costs nothing, but creates a nice atmosphere.

(Goes out to the audience, carrying a candle which he passes on to someone, asking him/her to blow it out.) Why don't you blow it out, you have nothing to lose. *(Moves up a few rows, where he disappears in the darkness. He lies down on the floor – music, a lot of sad music – suddenly, he raises up his head, which pops up from under the seats.)* It's me, me, who told Joan Miro that by painting idiotic circles, childish stars and sloppy stains one can make a lot of money...

SCENE FOUR

The Actor plays a musical instrument, ideally, a borrowed violin.

He plays, while making faces – faces are more important than the music!

He plays basically the same thing over and over – slowly moving forward…

(Suddenly.)

Pimp wouldn't be a pimp if he wasn't a pimp – that's logical.

(He plays and screams;

plays and sings;

plays and mouths – mute – as if singing;

speaks to himself:)

Yesterday I went to the fishing store, I saw on display a fishing rod with an inside hook, but they didn't have them in the store, and the display couldn't be de-constructed as it is planned for an entire month – why don't you come over later and ask again, the guy said – I bought a hook and three and half yards of thin line. I gave away the hook to a man at the bus stop, and I used the line to tie a pack of letters recommending me as an expert in areas I have no clue about. … *(Screaming.)* In the old days, we were taught not to " ask too many questions," to accept things as they were, without any protest, but also without any enthusiasm – that's how we were made. The results: we're surrounded by things we know nothing about, things we can't even see. To translate it into the language of art: we can register some phenomena without being able to judge them; we can look at them without being able to change them. The artists are familiar with that kind of auto-creating force because the creation itself is driven by it ('something' drives us to create what we create, and the aesthetic consciousness exists only on the pages of theoretical philosophers of the arts). Art plays its own chess game, while leaving us less and less satisfied (let's finally admit it!) with our contemporary art-making.

(Calms down, ideally.) Perhaps it happens because we are slowly entering the era of artistic disillusions, realizing that even our own consciousness is delusional. It's art, and particularly music as the most autonomous of all arts, that creates an ideal reflection of the world in which we live in, an ideal reflection of its antinomy. Perhaps it is through art that we will one day be able to learn about all the irrational things, things about which we usually learn too late to make any difference.

(Screaming.)

Perhaps it is contemporary music that will one day create some kind of other fields of hearing that which in our world exists above and beyond ourselves. Perhaps we finally will try to ask ourselves new questions, different questions, about the role and function of music in our lives, about the way that music exists, about the way that the human being exists vis-à-vis art and vice versa, the way that art exists vis-à-vis the human being.

(Darkness, or near darkness; calmly, as if reporting:)

In the corner of a dirty train car

a morose man was chewing on his fingernails

ogling

each passing figure

which appeared in the entryway of the train

next to him lay a pile of discarded newspapers

three or four days old

(that's how long his trip across the country lasted)

every few moments, he was grabbing one of them

immersing himself

in already memorized text

licking the same words

or words so similar to each other

that they had no meaning whatsoever

his crusty eyes starred into the paper

looking for truth that was no longer there

and when tired he tried to fall asleep

(first time in forty-eight hours)

resting

opening his mouth in spasmodic yawning

picking out leftover food from his gums

and flicking it with unusual dexterity

on the floor

drawing an elegant ballistic curve

(the best shooters

could be jealous of)

but he didn't fall asleep

vigilant

opening

one eye

or the other

falling into dull stupor

the kind

we wouldn't be able to find even in the animal kingdom

This man didn't know how to be himself

didn't understand the mask of social life

or cultural life

he was all alone in the world

possessed by his own thoughts

and drowning day after day

in the black river of biological sustenance

well-known to everyone

stripped of his dignity and his clothes

without honor

without a travel bag

without a future.

He was happy with the happiness of the drowned

and those who are not asked any questions

he had no intention to share

his happiness with anyone

disdaining everything that

wasn't it

even his fellow travelers who shared his misery

and perhaps

them even more than other people

whom he didn't understand

he never engaged in small talk or in any conversation

didn't ask anyone about anything

even what time it is

which he didn't care for anyways

he's been erasing from his memory everything

connected to life

keeping it at an arm's length

concentrating on a few muscles

that he recently strained

and the taste of food

that usurped his upper body

ravaged by the disease

left alone

to himself

dirty with the dirt of the antisocial life

sentenced and sentencing himself

to the misery of loneliness

and boundless despair

he put himself ahead of everything and everyone else

not because he was proud

but due to addling loneliness

which makes people believe only in that

which they experience themselves

Distrustful towards everyone

only once did he allow himself to talk about himself

with someone who like him had too much time on his hands

who asked him, out of boredom, how was he doing

and was charitable enough to listen to his answer

He talked for five or six hours

striving for precision

in describing everything he encountered

it was a dreary long story like rain outside the train window

which

on this day of grand self-presentation

was pouring profusely

– later he regretted his confession

but not because his interlocutor wasn't deserving

or attentive enough

but because

he told him everything as it was

without spicing or coloring anything

as if

he wanted to prove the tedious monotony of life

and after all

he could be suspected of it

I told you everything

– he said

but the essence of things is not here

it's elsewhere

even if you won't believe me

when I tell you

that I'm most bothered by loneliness

I'll lie

because I invented it for myself

I stick by it even today

when I suspect old age is creeping up on me

although in the end I don't even know if I'm thirty years old

or sixty

when I say

that I'm bothered by the lack of faith

I'll lie

because I recanted it myself

even though I don't know why

finally, when I say

that I'm bothered by poverty

it was me who made sure to nurture it

And so that's how he summed up himself

trying to save himself from the trappings of his own wretched confession

he wanted to take flight

how gladly he would flee his own life

if it didn't cost him any effort

which he avoided the most

he wanted to flee the fight

he never provoked

for which he had no strength

where will I find the strength without hope – he cried out

I haven't had it for a long time

the only thing I have is patience

but nothing good came out of it

patience is as useless

as everything else I've paraded around

– lost in my thoughts (equally useless as

everything else he did in the last few years) he didn't even
notice

when his listener left the train

leaving him again

alone

...

(Long pause.)

(He speaks:)

- nobody ever died of nausea
- I got terribly cold, but then, I warmed up again
- nothing will come out of it
- I saw you kissing this asshole
- why don't you hand it to me and I'll throw it over
- it's not your fucking business
- compluvium is nothing else, Ladies and Gentlemen, but the hole in the roof of the atrium that lets the light in
- the sycophant has a house and a chicken makes a noise
- Vania jumps – his record 2:18
- the pedipalps use their claws to catch their pray

- don't tell me, I know what I know
- Cathodoluminescence is a kind of luminescence caused by the beam of electors bombarding a luminescent material

(The Actor lies down anywhere, wimping, waiting…he starts speaking in a youthful voice and moves towards the voice of an old man, then back again, reverts to young voice:)

The consequences of recent socio-psychological and civilizational developments can be quite surprising to us in the not too distant future: if, indeed, the automatic mass production of goods will be as efficient as they claim it will be, it will reach a point of oversaturation, thus ensuring that we will need to amplify the need for and consumption of these goods. Needs will be manufactured. It's obvious that need and consumption will be economically dependent on supply, labor, material and capital. Even today, we can easily notice that the production of material goods exceeds the need for these goods; in order to be successful in any kind of economic endeavor, one needs to manufacture not just the goods, but also the needs. Naturally, these needs will be manufactured in a more and more artificial manner, following irrational rules with regards to man's real needs (even today, "others" know better what we need than we do – it's only a step away from educational determinism of man in the broadest sense: man as a product of needs that others have sentenced him to!)

Finally, I became a chef in luxury passenger trains. I cooked for rich assholes crossing our poor country in the first-class coaches. I cooked meals that even the worst pigs wouldn't touch, and for myself, in the back of the kitchen, I'd prepare the most fantastic gourmet meals: tail soup with parakeet meat, cotlets à la Lagerlöf with broccoli decorated with green radishes, and for dessert, dolce diplomatico with café au lait, with milk or without, depending on my current state of mind after the gluttony. Later, I started selling tapes with contemporary music, right from the sidewalks, one for five cents, and ten for thirty cents. Since nobody was buying them, I put an old cowboy hat in the front of the suitcase in which I kept the tapes. Rarely some beggar's change ended up in that hat. With my last pennies, I bought an expensive lottery ticket, which...

(He stops and returns to the main train of thought.)

Under the circumstances, it is unjustifiable – romantic and nonsensical even – to believe that free time is tied to the artistic life, the life of art, a connection with the most refined products of the human spirit. Unjustified also is the belief in the supremacy of man's needs, since even today we see that his cultural needs can be quite base, lowered to the coarsest tastes by an industry that specializes in manufacturing them on command. There is no doubt that the man of industrialized spirit remains under the pressure of that industry; what's more, he becomes its slave.

> *(Suddenly.)* ...with my last pennies, I bought an expensive lottery ticket, which, of course, as it was easy to predict, didn't win me anything.

It's true that in some narrow capacity, a man can still decide some things, but in the end, seen statistically, he limits himself to consumption of values imposed on him by others. This typical-for-modern-man depersonalization and uniformization of so-called artistic products parallels ideally the image of the captive mind. The recipient is left with no choice but to receive, consume, devour everything that's designed for him; since all of his needs are programmed according to predetermined rules, he can't object because these needs are manufactured outside of his knowledge and his participation – although, for his own good.

(He escapes the stage; appears again as if he were a stranger, a different man; performs mundane household tasks – as if he were in his home; he gives the impression that he has lived here for years; he is preoccupied with himself, his tasks, fixing something, improving; he is bored…)

SCENE FIVE

Musical Composition.

(Music; the Actor puts away the props; it should be apparent that this scene wraps up the show.)

(Seriously – lecturing.) In our époque it will be very difficult to salvage all of the values that we came to treasure so much. Historically speaking, this process of the depersonalization and uniformization of social life is inevitable. Only taking some kind of detached, abstract or metaphysical position will allow one to ponder questions like: what interesting possibilities for man does the future hold, on what scale will he be able to express himself? Today's art – please, note: art has always been ahead of its time – today's art is proof of the impuissance of artistic forces and the superiority of social forces. For years now, we have been reading in journals and newspapers articles written by the most brilliant minds of our times about the lack of profound emotional foundation and lack of reflection in our modern lives: today's man thinks and feels completely differently than his parents or grandparents did. Both the emotional and the reflective aspects of life penetrate only the surface of his thinking matter, and man more often than not consents to what happens to him, no longer wasting his time on heretofore important quests for the ethical motivations behind his actions. In the spiritual life, however, these ethical motivations have always taken the first place; let me remind you that in the past the thinkers, the scientists and the artists went to great pains, often resulting in their own self-destruction, to convince people of the value of art and its judgments.

Shaping the identity of a modern man, that is, in our case, the identity of an artist and his audience, will depend on the level of independence that modern man will be able to maintain towards himself. Modern man will have to achieve distance from his needs (both "the natural" and the manufactured ones), since only in this way will he be able to cling to some shred of hope that he still means something. On the other hand, his compliance with the world of conspicuous consumption, compliance with this new form of slavery (in this case, spiritual slavery) will inevitably lead to the annihilation of his identity and individuality. It will reduce him to a common statistic, that is, to a small digit in a large enslaved human mass, which innocently – what can one man alone do after all? – will drown in spiritual malaise, delighted only with its own existence, destroyed by the dark forces of hopelessness, waiting for its inevitable end.

QUARTET FOR FOUR ACTORS

Quartet for Four Actors. Dir. by Beata Fudalej. Photo by Adam Bondarowicz, 2009. Courtesy of "Grupa Dochodzeniowa." Międzynarodowy Festiwal Ensemble in Książ (International Ensemble Fesival). Actors from the "Grupa Dochodzeniowa"– from left: Mateusz Ławrynowicz, Dorota Kuduk (guest), Jarosław Sacharski, Agata Sasinowska.

Dramatis Personae

ANDRZEJ/A/ANDREW
(VIOLINIST I)

JANUSZ/J/JOHN
(VIOLINIST II)

MIKOLAJ/N/NICHOLAS
(VIOLA PLAYER)

ZYGMUNT/Z/SIGMUND
(CELLIST)

SCENE ONE

The beginning.

Four actors stand on the table, creating a frozen sculpture which nonetheless, sings:

For about one minute each actor sings a different motif:

ANDREW   _ _ _ _ _---------

JOHN   ----------_ _ _ _ _

NICHOLAS   _____---------

SIGMUND   ----------_ _ _ _

The length of each element is very different, thanks to which the sum should create polyphony

    now, humming, very quietly!!!

SCENE TWO

all four of the actors are breaking stones

each does it in a different rhythm

each does it in a different place

model A – twenty seconds

model B – twenty seconds

model A' – twenty seconds / it has to resemble model A

an example of a rhythmic model

model A

A .   .   .   .
        .   .   .   etc.

J .   ...
        ...   etc.

```
M .        .          .                        .        .          .
          .        .          .                etc.
Z  ..                          ..                                      ..
              ..                               etc.
```

completely out of sync!

model B

```
A  .              .                      .                    .          .
         .        .......              .
J  .... . .....                  .          .          .          .          .
         .        .          .          .          .
M  .        .          .          .          .          .          .          .
         .        .          .          .          .
S  .        .                  .                  .          .          .
    ...............  .                  .                  .
```

very measured acceleration and slowing down

SCENE THREE

"Metamusic" of a special kind –

ppp

– about 30 seconds (up to 50 seconds max)

A: *(Harmonica – very softly, almost silent.)*

J: *(Murmuring – without opening his mouth.)*

N: *(Falsetto – as quietly as possible.)*

Z: *(Whistling, subtly.)*

models:

```
FIRST:              ...............''''''''''''''''''''''...............---------
    ------
THEN:  -----------...............---------------'''''''''''''''''''''''-----------
    --
```

THEN: ''''''''''''''''''''---------------.................
                                    ''''''''''''''''''''''''''''''

(Finally – each in his own rhythm.)

    o-------------

       o--------------------

           o---

  o----------------- o--

                o-----------------

          o---

       (etc.)

(=silence filled with sounds coming from nowhere.)

SCENE FOUR

JOHN is carefully dressing SIGMUND up. NICHOLAS jumps on JOHN's shoulder and sits on his back, etc. JOHN continues very calmly. He can murmur something to himself, like: 'it'll be nicer like that,' 'you won't get cold this way,' 'this is more flattering,' etc.

pantomime

for about one minute

JOHN

and

NICHOLAS

i m p r o v i s e

SIGMUND nearly limp, lifeless.

ANDREW is reading poetry, quietly, but clearly. Away from everyone.

SCENE FIVE

SIGMUND and NICHOLAS exit.

ANDREW: They're gone. We can finally talk!

JOHN: What about?

ANDREW: I don't know. Maybe about them.

JOHN: About them? They're dull.

ANDREW: The taller one seems fishy.

JOHN: Yeah, more fishy than the other one. And horribly self-important.

ANDREW: Hey, maybe he is important.

JOHN: If he were, he wouldn't have to pretend.

ANDREW: That's true. I don't have to pretend.

JOHN: You? What about you? Do you know who you are?

ANDREW: *(Whispers something in JOHN's ear. They both laugh / more laughter / more gestures, after a while:)*

JOHN: I don't remember his name.

ANDREW: Who?

JOHN: If I knew *who*, I would have told you. Something starting with 'sp.' Something common.

ANDREW: Spinach.

JOHN: No, not Spinach. Spinach is an uncommon last name.

ANDREW: There was a soccer player named Spinach. He played defense – I think.

JOHN: Public defender.

ANDREW: No, defender of the oppressed.

JOHN: Anyone can be called Spinach.

ANDREW: Anyone sure can, but doesn't have to.

JOHN: I got it. It didn't begin with 'sp,' it began with 'zp.'

ANDREW: Bro, stop thinking about it and it will come to you. *(He continues explaining something to JOHN: 'you know, my old mate,' etc. something like that – for a long time.)*

JOHN: *(Suddenly very loud.)* No, shut up!

ANDREW: Seriously, I swear to you.

JOHN: That's the darnedest thing! *(They both leave.)*

SCENE SIX

The actors sit on four chairs, playing a QUARTET silently. music stands in front of them, with blank pages.

Only their hands move playing

a string quartet   *for about fifteen seconds*

they play and sing (humming.)

a strange, modern string quartet   *for about fifteen seconds*

they play and sing, but in one direction – to the left (Like in a mirror.) continuation of the previous quartet
                              for about fifteen seconds

with their hands behind their backs, they hum the quartet long flat notes, lyric part   *for about fifteen seconds*

the above scene lasts for a total of about one minute

SCENE SEVEN

For about two minutes...

Solo

SIGMUND

      is left alone

                s l o w l y

he's doing

a crossword puzzle

–   *a very enigmatic one*

            he can read (pretending to write,
            filling out the crossword puzzle with his pencil...)

Something like:

SIGMUND:

"Australian philosopher from sixteenth century – three
letters – starts with 'H,' third letter 'Y.' Hay? hey? hij? – I
don't know. I have no idea." "Let's see – three down: a
small town known for an assault on its barman – sixty-six
letters, starts with 'H,' Northern Wales. That's a difficult
one." "Philosophical theory, promoted by Jane Fonda
among others – ends with ISM – eight letters – shit,
that's difficult too." "Sexual self-depravation – ends with
'A' – also the name of the American Navy ship that sank
with record speed." "OK, let's try this one: activist – starts
with 'D' – maybe 'defender' – no, one letter is missing."
"Legendary pirate leader – that's a difficult one – eleven
letters, sixth 'B'" "Famous saying of Prague bridge players
after they lose the first round without trumps – five letters
– I don't know, I don't know. How am I supposed to
know something like that?" "The inventor of the Haymore
valve – seven letters – first 'H' – penultimate 'R' – I got

it! Haymore – OK, great, but you do have to be a valve expert to guess that one. What's a humanist supposed to do? His interests don't include valves. What's he supposed to do?" "An inhabitant of the mountains – starts with 'H' – highlander – yes, no, it doesn't fit, the second letter is 'I'"

(He speaks, quieter and quieter, and more and more to himself...)

SCENE EIGHT

For about forty seconds

A group psychosis

e v e r y o n e i s l o o k i n g f o r s o m e t h i n g i n h i s p o c k e t s

develop this scene:

one starts to look (his own rhythm, let's say it's SIGMUND) – then, the next one (at a different speed, let's say it's ANDREW) – the third one starts looking ALSO – this ALSO needs to be arranged! (JOHN, for example) – the fourth one (let's say NICHOLAS) starts helping SIGMUND (they start to look in each other's pockets)

etc.

etc.

etc.

> *it's a lighter, which eventually one of them ignites – he wants to help to light someone else's cigarette –*

> *but:*

> *there is no one there*

End of scene.

SCENE NINE

music is coming from an audio tape

AZIONE A DUE

the actors

play

on harmonicas

in this way:

they walk around the stage

they crouch near the source of the sound, that is, the loudspeaker

and

add one note – very discreetly

to make it look as if the note was part of the recorded music

they try to find an appropriate sound

they sit with their backs to the audience

(their faces and harmonicas should be hidden from the audience's view)

the point is to supplement the music with one long sound

coming from the stage

after a half-minute break, they make another sound, etc.

total time for the scene: they do it for about five minutes and thirty seconds

SCENE TEN

strictly musical

l a b y r i n t h

   for about two minutes

each actor reads starting at a different place

```
                                                    TO
SC    a battle scream              SIG
THU   imitated thunder                          COU

PAN   roar of the panther                   STU
LIE   lie down quickly on the floor SCR    BR
TO        aching tooth                 SIG              GI
SI        siren                     BR          SC
SCR   scream / inarticulate sounds/    THU  COU      SFF
WH    whisper / vaguely /         WH      SU
BR        breathe                 WHI   TO    FIZ  STO
SIG   sigh                  CR          sFF GI
GI        giggle            THU         PAN  LIE
CL    clap                              BR
COU   cough                 LIE         WHI       STO
WHI   whimper               CR                 FIZ
CR        cry                   THU               SCR
FIZ   fizzle                THU
sFF   whisper with a sudden sFF in the middle WH
STO   stomp                             TO
```

SCENE ELEVEN

all four actors

this scene is strictly musical – and it lasts for about 40 seconds

elements:

RU – rustle of paper (*copy paper*)

DB – deep breaths (*asthmatic*)

WH – whistling in one's sleep

notes:

ANDREW:	RU			DB			WH		
JOHN:		RU				DB			WH
NICHOLAS:	RU		DB		WH				
SIGMUND:			RU		DB			WH	

SCENE TWELVE

Spoken scene, with rhythmic beat

ANDREW: to make a faster delivery *(8 times)* – by telegram *(7 times)* – addressee's signature required *(6 times)* – delivery of the telegram *(5 times)* – when the addressee has a phone *(4 times)* – when he owns a teleprinter *(5 times)* – before the telegram *(6 times)* – a day before it is delivered *(7 times)*

JOHN: we reach an extreme *(8 times)* – total serialization *(7 times)* – and absolute modalism *(6 times)* – if in major points *(7 times)* – a combination of the material *(8 times)* etc. *(From the beginning)*

NICHOLAS: pay your membership dues regularly, hey *(6 times)* – financial obligations *(7 times)* – and consequences, hey-ho *(8 times)* – irregular payment of your membership fees *(7 times)* – sanctions will be imposed *(8 times)* etc. *(From the beginning.)*

SIGMUND: overcooked *(9 times)* – stuffed *(8 times)* – encrusted *(7 times)* – and drained *(6 times)* – stuffed *(5 times)* – and picked clean *(6 times)* – spring chicken *(7 times)* – unsalted *(8 times)* etc. *(From the beginning)*

whispering mysteriously, mumbling

total for about one minute and twenty seconds

in the form of absolute 4-voice

SCENE THIRTEEN

All four actors are onstage, far away from each other, but still talking.

ANDREW: Let me tell you, gentlemen, what happened to me today. I was looking out the window this morning...

NICHOLAS: *(Interrupting ANDREW.)* Something much *better* happened to me. I drive out of my garage, turn left and guess what I see....

JOHN: *(Rudely.)* Whatever! I'm in bed with a girl – at her place – we've just met, and suddenly, the door opens...

SIGMUND: *(Feverishly.)* Yes, yes. You can't predict anything. That's great! If there were no surprises, there would be nothing to talk about.

ANDREW: So, I look out the window – it was raining, only so lightly – ...

NICHOLAS: *(Interrupting ANDREW again, in the same way.)* I turn and what do I see? A completely naked guy lying on the hood of my car.

JOHN: *(With mean-spirited curiosity.)* On the hood of your car? Why?

NICHOLAS: On the hood. On the hood of my car.

SIGMUND: You were driving wearing a hood?

NICHOLAS: The hood of the car.

JOHN: You can hoodwink anyone if you wanted to.

SIGMUND: But eventually, everything will come out. The police will sniff it out, before there's even a scent.

ANDREW: That's their job. But they're too obvious, too visible.

JOHN: They should walk around hearing hoods.

SIGMUND: Everyone should be walking around wearing hoods.

ANDREW: The number of crimes would climb.

JOHN: Criminal activity is always accompanied by – as Samuel Hozenduft, from Yale University noticed – the increased prosperity of a given country.

NICHOLAS: So the stripped guy screams at me to take him – yes – to take him to...

ANDREW: Stripped? You meant to say: broke.

JOHN: They used to call a poor man broke.

SIGMUND: To quote a poet:

> Broke has pants full of dope

ANDREW: But for an idea, he don't mind getting the rope

NICHOLAS: Hanged man shits with no hope

SIGMUND: Too many pervs in the town of Lope

JOHN: *(Warning them.)* I've just met her, but we've clicked so it went really fast. So, we're just starting to have some fun, when the door opens. A guy comes in and says: 'Say, when you're done, could you please answer one question for me? In what way...'

SIGMUND: *(Interrupting.)* I'm sorry to interrupt. Were you on top of her, or was she on top of you?

JOHN: What does it matter?

NICHOLAS: A man's position matters a lot. That broke guy, for example...

ANDREW: It was raining, ever so lightly. I opened the window to let the fresh air in...

SIGMUND: Now that's what we call a mutual exchange. You release not-so-fresh air into the world, the world gives you fresh air in return.

SIGMUND: *(To NICHOLAS.)* When we consider all the pollution, it can be the other way around. For example: I opened the window and let the stench of civilization into my apartment.

NICHOLAS: Soon enough, our breath will smell like fresh car smoke.

SIGMUND: Exhale now, show me – your wife or girlfriend will say – yes, now I know where you were. You went to the church.

NICHOLAS: To the empty church.

SIGMUND: Yes, indeed. Empty, with no people.

ANDREW: I opened the window. <u>Different</u> air entered the room and all of a sudden, I felt that someone was standing behind me.

JOHN: Who?

ANDREW: I turned around, but he was gone.

JOHN: You imagined it.

NICHOLAS: Might be a progressive mental illness. It begins with mild hallucinations and soon enough, we all know how it ends.

ANDREW: Do you think I'm crazy? Do you think I would be able to tell you this story if there was something wrong with me?

NICHOLAS: Who knows? Crazies are cunning.

SIGMUND: I knew one such a fellow. He faked his craziness to escape the draft. Didn't work no place, sold something here and here. Then, he advanced.

JOHN: He or his illness?

SIGMUND: Both simultaneously. Once, he spend his entire paycheck to buy socks.

JOHN: But you said that he didn't work no place. Whose paycheck then?

SIGMUND: Not his of course. He wasn't crazy. His twin brother's. You know, he was quite taken by... *(They start talking among themselves. Only bits and pieces of the conversation can be heard: "He wasn't all that crazy," "Sure, but who was supposed to guess that," "They didn't want to believe him," etc.)*

SCENE FOURTEEN

Choir.

Three men sing. One stands with his back to the audience and pseudo-conducts them.

Attempt at composition.

About 2 minutes.

REACTIONS: Like at the choir rehearsal.

They sing a bit; then, they're stopped by the "conductor," who corrects someone: "Sing higher, not too much, just a little, from the top." – They stop again, talk about passion, they need more passion. – They start again, wrong again. – The "conductor" switches – they start again – wrong again – from the top. The new "conductor" has a temper – he screams: "Do you have any idea how you sound? Do you want me to tell you how?" – Again, from the top, they go further. Slowly, the text of the song emerges, although they don't sing all of it – they give up and move on to the next scene.

Text of the song:

When that I was and a little tiny boy[1]

……………………………both of my hands

……………………………………………stank

………………………………………………like a putrid bok choy

………………………………/oy/ but soon over was my

………………………misery [*the conductor corrects them: miesery, not misery*]

………………/misery/ and now, one of them stinks like a celery.

SCENE FIFTTEEN

One minute and 30 seconds

Collage:

ANDREW: whistles

JOHN: talks

NICHOLAS: screams

SIGMUND: sings

About 1 minute

Whistling: *(Whatever.)*

Talking: "to be oneself one has to not want to be oneself"
    – "didn't I work hard enough, and what? what came of
    it?" – "any idiot can confirm it, it's all clear" – "do we
    have something to say, or don't we" – "what if one were
    to approach this from a completely different angle" – "we

---

1   This line is taken from Shakespeare's *Twelfth Night.*

don't have a right to judge anybody – hang them – yes – but for God's sake – never to judge!" – *(Twenty sentences like that.)*

Screaming: "I don't want to" – " I'll no longer allow it" – "it's a scandal" – "I know what you're all thinking" – "you're thinking it's easy, but it's not easy, not at all" – "I'll show you all" – "why me, why me?" *(Some of the sentences are addressed to the ones who whistle or sing.)*

Singing: *(Whatever. Ideally, something as idiotic as "The next time I'll come to you wearing armor" or something like that.)*

SCENE SIXTEEN

JOHN: *(Exits.)*

ANDREW: The one that just left – he's a nancy.

SIGMUND: John?

ANDREW: No, not a john; a queer. But I've got nothing in common with him.

SIGMUND: And what can real men have in common with each other? Well, maybe a girlfriend.

ANDREW: If the two men have her in common, then, everybody has her.

SIGMUND: She can't do everybody. You overestimate women. Two – that's possible, if she alternates them. I knew a girl like that *(Whispering something.)*.

SCENE SEVENTEEN

C o n v e r s a t i o n with their mouths full.

Roles:

ANDREW: football [or soccer]

JOHN: vodka [alcohol]

About 2 minutes   NICHOLAS: cards [gambling]

SIGMUND: hookers

All four = = = all four 'real' men

First:

They talk, each discusses his OWN topic

they don't let the others talk

although they speak relatively calmly

Then:

They begin to eat / slowly, one after another – not all of them together / and they talk – intensely, as they stuff their mouths – their language gets stronger, their arguments more persuasive, they start yelling / when one of them chokes, the others grab the opportunity to talk about their own problems, etc.

Subjects:

A: match   – why his team lost

B: vodka   – should have mixed it up last night

C: cards   – ran out of luck

D: hookers   – could have given me a clamp

Finally:

All of their frustrations, complaints, pessimism, etc. come out.

SCENE EIGHTEEN

Solo scene

ANDREW

arranges the other three men, who are completely limp. He arranges them into a 'pedestal'

steps all over them

fixes here and there

stands on them again – more secure

gives a short speech

ANDREW: Ivan Fyodorovich was a rich man. When something got stuck in between his teeth, he called on a dentist from the nearby town. When something got stuck in his eye, he asked his servant Vanya to tell him everything he sees. When he got a girl pregnant, he married her off with a huge dowry. He didn't care about money, about what other people thought about him, about anything or anyone. He only had one wish. He wanted everybody to go to hell. *(The 'pedestal' falls apart and* ANDREW *falls on the ground upon the words 'go to hell'.)*

The scene takes place in darkness

It takes about 40 seconds to prepare for it.

The scene takes about 1 minute and 40 seconds.

SCENE NINETEEN

Solo

JOHN

1 minute 10 seconds

Pseudo-language grammar lesson

"Madness!"

He talks:
"it's simple really – conjugate the verb in Buyayak PRIMHIM" "I PRIMHAM" "we PRIMHAMY" "you PRIMHAMU" "she PRIMHAMS" "easy, clean and clear – the author is right: this language is really attractive" "only 3500 people speak Buyayak – 100 of them don't

speak it because they're still babies so they don't speak yet, and 120 no longer speak it because they forgot how to talk in their language and only use the official language. Language experts don't speak it because they prefer Ahalalay, which has an easier grammar. Experts don't like to work too hard nowadays – easier grammar! It's easier not to talk at all, but what are you to do if you're a man?" "Let's continue. In Buyayak, mom is MOM, easy, you say, MOM! – Oh, MOMS – MOMMY." [*He speaks quieter, only fragments can be heard.* "PRIMHAM MAMEN, PRIMHAMY NOMEN OMEN, NAHOMEN MAOMEN HAM, HAM MAMY, HYMEN HIMEN MAHOMY, HAMEN HANUMY, NAHUMEN NAHOME PRIMHASCH," etc. *(He walks away, fragments of his monologue can be heard. He disappears. The end.)*

SCENE TWENTY

1 minute 40 seconds

Solo

NICHOLAS

He is preparing for an interview for the job of TV anchor, or he just talks about it...

Like this:
"Any man can be a TV anchor, if he has no criminal record, is over 35 years old, and has appropriate citizenship papers, and if he can talk" – "that's the first step" – "second step: he needs to know how to read – everyone thinks they know how to read, but it's all bluff" – "he needs to know how to read difficult texts, like Husserl, Ingarden or Putrament" – "he needs to know how to learn to read absurd texts, tongue twisters" – "like for example: PETER PIPER PICKED A PECK OF PICKLED PEPPERS. Or something like that: A PECK OF PICKLED PEPPERS PETER PIPER PICKED. Or even something as simple as: If PETER PIPER PICKED

A PECK OF PICKLED PEPPERS. Or even better, something that goes like: WHERE'S THE PECK OF PICKLED PEPPERS PETER PIPER PICKED? – the fact that most TV anchors can't read a simple sentence from a piece of paper shouldn't stand in a way of making sure that someone else – in the future – who wants to bore us to death with his reading should do so masterfully – so, let us continue: A PECK OF PICKLED PEPPERS PETER PIPER PICKED, etc." *(Fading...)*

SCENE TWENTY-ONE

Group scene

Actors:

Everyone does whatever, but:

They discuss it among themselves,

making arrangements,

they argue,

fight over nothing,

chaos

busy work.

Fragments of conversation:

"are you coming?" – "no, I'll come over later" – "I have time" – "no rush" – "not now" – "can we postpone it" – "let's just get it done now" – "what's the rush" – "take it with you, or, better yet, leave it here"

Impression

They are supposed to go somewhere

it's time to go

they are supposed to take something with them

or: leave it

Who, what, why and what for

we don't know

/ this should be the essence of this scene /

It lasts about 1 minute

SCENE TWENTY-TWO

All four actors sitting together, randomly or prearranged, it's hard to say.

SIGMUND: *(Pensive.)* I don't know how it came to it, how it happened, but the world no longer makes sense.

ANDREW: Our sense of reality is mechanical. Modern man has lost touch with reality.

JOHN: *(With emphasis.)* Lost touch – without touch our lives are deprived of what's most important.

They think, silently. Pause.

NICHOLAS: I ran into Kazek yesterday. Darn it, he looked old. And no longer as elegant as he used to.

JOHN: *(With emphasis, without paying any attention to NICHOLAS.)* The loss of metaphysics in our lives weakens our sense of existence.

ANDREW: I agree, our lives are devoid of depth.

SIGMUND: It tears us apart, we're stuck between what's important and what's imperceptible. That's a real tragedy.

NICHOLAS: *(Persistently.)* Tragedy, tragedy. Do you know why I knew that there was something going on with Kazek? Dandruff! He always had really bad dandruff, but then, he met the woman of his life, and the dandruff is gone. Not a flake! I saw it with my own eyes!

SIGMUND: *(Calmly.)* The world ceases to have a meaning, and everything we do transcendentally becomes mechanized.

ANDREW: Mechanized and multiplied by the modern man's modal relationship to the world surrounding him.

JOHN: Man's relationship to his death also became modal.

NICHOLAS: *(Interrupting him absent-mindedly.)* Woman – that's a real power. She even managed to deal with his dandruff, and how fast she did it! How fast!

JOHN: *(To NICHOLAS.)* Dandruff, you see, seborrheic dermatitis is a common, inflammatory skin condition that causes flaky, white to yellowish scales to form on oily areas such as the scalp. Infrequent hygiene can exacerbate this unpleasant condition, and woman can be considered an antidote to that cause. If we didn't elevate women... ein Weib bleibt nur Weib – to quote Emanuel Rosshaar. Translating literally *(With contempt.)* for you: a woman is just a woman. *(Returns to the previous subject.)* Man's modal relationship to his death evokes a new sense of reality.

ANDREW: Unfortunately, nowadays, this new sense of reality has been devoid of all emotions.

JOHN: And that's how we return to the point of departure: our self, which is no longer ours, and no longer self.

NICHOLAS: *(Catching up now, to JOHN.)* What are you saying? A woman can do anything with a man, anything she wants! *(Getting upset, and carried away.)* You should read Ferruccio Mantovani's L'influenza della femini alle forze creative del grandi artisti. How many masterful artworks were created under the influence of women!

JOHN: *(Furious that he's gotten sucked into the conversation.)* Yes, but you were kind enough to insert women into a very different context! You talked about women and their ability to rid men of dandruff. Don't deny it now! Let me quote your own words: "She even managed to deal with his dandruff, and how fast she did it! How fast!" I don't believe that Mantovani's book mentions anything about your absurd, irrational approach to this matter.

ANDREW: *(Unclear to whom he is speaking.)* I think that...

NICHOLAS: *(Interrupting him.)* I've heard you talking nonsense like that many times before. You think you know life, don't you? You know Kazek, right?

ANDREW: No, I've never had the pleasure of meeting him.

NICHOLAS: Who's saying it's a pleasure to meet him? I asked you if you know him.

ANDREW: No, I don't.

NICHOLAS: *(To JOHN.)* You see, he doesn't know what's going on, but wants to talk. You need to know how to talk. Your friend...excuse me, what's your name?

JOHN: My name is Waldo Manuree. Two e's.

NICHOLAS: Mr. Manuree, let's return to our conversation. What's your opinion of Kazek? I think he's an all right guy, but a bit of a son-of-a-bitch.

SIGMUND: Excuse me, what did you just say?

NICHOLAS: I wasn't talking to you. He seems like an educated man but you need to explain everything to him. Loser, a complete loser.

JOHN: I have to agree with you there.

NICHOLAS: Loserland.

JOHN: You hit the bull's eye with that.

NICHOLAS: *(Getting excited.)* Loser-schmoozer!

JOHN: Bravo! You're astonishing!

NICHOLAS: It was nice talking to you gentlemen, but I have to go now. Bye. *(He exits.)*

JOHN: Bye. *(Pause.)* Gentlemen! Let us not despair. At least part of our society retains a healthy, proactive relationship to the world.

SIGMUND: You mean this moron?

JOHN: He's a really nice man. He touched mc with his directness, which you obviously are lacking. And he's educated.

SIGMUND: Him?! Educated?!

JOHN: I want to remind you how effortlessly he just quoted a well-known book by Mantovani, though I've got to admit, the connection between Mantovani and dandruff was a bit unfortunate. You know, I got scared there for a moment that he'd start talking in Italian, and my Italian is so-so.

SIGMUND: *(Interrupting him.)* You got scared of that imbecile?!

ANDREW: Not an imbecile, not an imbecile – excuse me! At a few instances in our discussion, this gentleman whom you call imbecile, revealed an exquisite rhetorical talent. I would go even further and suggest that his participation in our debate enlivened what had started as quite a pessimistic exchange. Whatever you'd say, he moved it in a more optimistic direction.

SIGMUND: *(Pause.)* Well, I have to agree with you after all. Since he didn't make a good first impression, we were all prone – all of us were prone – to dismiss his greatness, his genius way of interrupting our conversation at exactly the moment when it got the most intense.

ANDREW: Indeed, if he just wanted *(From now on speaking in fragments, all of them, ANDREW, SIGMUND and JOHN.)* he could get a doctorate, what do I know, maybe even become a full professor...maybe not...but yes...yes! yes! ...indeed, indeed...natural born orator...he really can overwhelm you with the power of his personality...(etc., etc.)

SCENE TWENTY-THREE

About 50 seconds

All of them play harmonicas

Long notes

IN – inhale

EX – exhale

It goes something like that:

AN:	EX	IN	EX	IN	EX	etc.
JOHN:		IN	EX	IN	EX	etc.
NICK:	EX	IN	EX	IN	EX	etc.
SIG:			EX	IN	EX	etc.

SCENE TWENTY-FOUR

ANDREW: I think it's time that we ponder the meaning of music as such. I think that in music, the most important aspects are the transcendental ones, the ones that go beyond music, but also in fact, consist it.

JOHN: It's an old-fashioned approach. I think that in music *(Clearly and with emphasis.)* the most important aspects are the ones which it could do without.

SIGMUND: I don't know exactly what *(To JOHN.)* mister Professor here means, but I agree with him completely. Transcendence is the only thing that counts. Only transcendence. Only *(To JOHN.)* – don't interrupt me, please! – only transcendence.

NICHOLAS: Gentlemen, gentlemen, gentlemen! We can't talk like that about art. Please, allow me to insert a little order into our conversation. *(To ANDREW.)* You dismiss transcendence – don't deny it! *(Yelling.)* You dismiss it! *(To JOHN.)* You talk about the elements of music which it cannot do *(Laughing.)* without. *(Furious.)* Who the hell do you think I am, a moron? I've been watching you for a while now. You always say utter nonsense. It should be punishable by law – by whipping, that would do it.

SIGMUND: I'm all for whipping. We all have been whipped, but not with a lash or bullwhip – and that makes all the difference.

JOHN: *(Calmly.)* I don't see any difference, and I'll tell you gentlemen, the way I was being whipped... nobody was ever whipped like that. *(To ANDREW with ecstasy.)* Man, those were the days.

ANDREW: They were, but they're over now. *(To JOHN.)* Times have changed and so did music. As a matter of fact, I could care less about transcendence.

SIGMUND: Don't fuck with me. You care a lot, that's all you ever talk about. It's your [f] obsession.

NICHOLAS: *(Like before.)* Gentlemen, gentlemen. Not like this, you can't do it like this. *(Fast.)* That is, you can, but ought not to. That is, you ought to, but it's unfitting. That is, it's fitting, but not for everyone. For me, for instance, it's fitting.

JOHN: What's fitting? Are you hallucinating? Your dentures got loose, not fitting? Go see your dentist, don't waste our time. I've had my eyes in you for a while now.

ANDREW: Eyes on you, not eyes in you. Tear in the eyes, stink in the air, and so on. Some forget even how to speak properly. He mumbles and he's all happy about it.

JOHN: I'm not all happy about anything. I take everything seriously. *(To NICHOLAS.)* I take everything very seriously.

NICHOLAS: What for? What the heck for? You don't take, you chew – and that's a big difference.

SIGMUND: It's all the same. Screw up or screw down – it's all the same. I could give you more examples like that.

ANDREW: Me too, but that's not the point. The point is...

JOHN: *(Singing.)*

ANDREW: That's nice. I didn't know you have a voice.

NICHOLAS: Any adult who votes has a voice. That's the way it is. You won't change it. *(Pause, with emphasis.)* You can shit all over yourself, but you won't change it.

SIGMUND: I'm glad we're back on the subject.

JOHN: In Mahler's music, everything is foggy-like. He's a great composer. Each time I come in contact with his art, it's like a celebration.

JOHN: All you ever do is celebrate. You should try working once in a while too.

NICHOLAS: Every job is honorable. Even the old toilet lady.

ANDREW: That's not a job.

NICHOLAS: *(Sharp.)* I don't know what toilets you like to grace with your presence, but the ones that I go to are clean, and it's a heck of a job to keep them that way. Even if you can't always tell how much work it was.

JOHN: People can make shit out of anything.

SIGMUND: Yes, man – hu-man – it sounds gross. To think of it: shit, urine, mucus, spit…

NICHOLAS: *(Energetically.)* Let's get back to our subject matter. Let's take the old toilet lady, or as they say, the lavatory attendant…

ANDREW: Give it a rest, won't you? It's a damn perversion. I prefer to take them younger, when they're in their prime – before they wither away.

JOHN: Take it when they give it to you – that's my motto.

SIGMUND: Every idiot knows that. You don't need a motto for that.

NICHOLAS: Mottos, as in mo to sos. Nonetheless, I'd like to return to the subject matter. As I already said, in music, the most important elements are the ones which it could do without.

JOHN: But it's _my_ thesis!

NICHOLAS: Yes? I don't recall. So, to sum it up: the most important elements are the ones which it could _not_ do without.

ANDREW: You mean, time, space, and matter.

SIGMUND: _(Sitting in the pose of Rodin's 'Thinker'.)_ The worse thing is that the modern man has no time. Not much space either. And matter – I can't come up with anything about matter.

NICHOLAS: Matter appears when there is oil.

JOHN: In a few years oil will rule over everything.

ANDREW: Yes, but I don't think that the oil – its supply – will influence the development of modern music.

SIGMUND: This discussion has gotten very interesting. We touched on many important subjects, indeed. _(Freudian slip.)_ Time to s-oil it up.

ANDREW: Yap, it's getting la-oil-te.

SIGMUND: I'll sum it up in one sentence. _(With emphasis.)_ The most important is intention.

NICHOLAS: Yes, intention. _(Moves on to the next scene.)_

SCENE TWENTY-FIVE

Final scene

A n t i p h o n a [tape]

7 minutes and 17 seconds

All four

0-2 – all four disappear

2-3 – they appear like shadows

3-4:30 – they sing together murmuring – from different locations on the stage

4:30-6 – they appear and disappear one by one like shadows

6-7:17 – they return to the very first position (to SCENE ONE) – it's the beginning of the entire composition

As the music gets softer –

They freeze in the poses

    of sculpture…

    which they formed at the beginning

    mute monument

It lasts about 15 seconds!

SCENARIO FOR THREE ACTORS

Scenario for Three Actors. Directed by Mikołaj Grabowski. Photo by Anna Włoch.
Courtesy of the author, 1998. Teatr Stu [Stu Theatre]. From the left: Andrzej
Grabowski, Mikolaj Grabowski and Jan Peszek.

I ALLEGRO

FIRST

(Alone and silent for a while; suddenly.) Ha! He had it
coming! Every idiot wants to outshine every other idiot!
Stun everyone with his brilliance, no matter what! Great
artist, he is, right! He invites a mob – excuse me, the
audience – and makes a happening! And when I ask him,
what is it exactly that he's doing, he replies that he doesn't
know yet, but it will *come* to him at the last minute! It
will come to him! What can possibly *come* to that moron!
He says: Oh, I don't need a director, it's not theatre. It's
a situation, which will just *come to him, come* out. Come
out! To him! *(Takes a pause and calms himself.)* A director
is needed even for the simplest, dumbest things. School
recitals, fashion shows, even funerals! Of course, I'm not
pushy. I just want to help. He's too dumb to even know
he needs a good director. And I happen to have directed
this and that: an opera and an operetta, an oratorio to
remember the victims – and of course, before that, one to
celebrate the victors – the students at school recitals and,
naturally, the classicists. Even a bank robbery needs to
be directed. Yes, it has to be directed and acted out, each
move and each gesture, someone has to be in control.
That's the director's role. *(He doesn't notice that he begins
to rhyme, so he speaks without rhyming, on the border between
prose and poetry.)* Even a heist! And the raid, of course,
too, and political provocation, the enthusiasm of the
crowds, the success of the spectacle – everything needs to
be directed, everything, everything – otherwise, nothing
will come out of it. *(Getting excited.)* Chaos and confusion
will come out! Shit will come out!

SECOND

(Entering on the FIRST's last words.) Will you **come out**
with me for a walk? I have two brief errands to run –
really brief – and then, I'd like to discuss with you the
relationship between music and drama. I believe that
drama doesn't need music, just like music doesn't need
drama. We can talk about it while we walk! You know,

I'm an idealist, and I'd like to keep it that way! I know, I know, composers can occasionally make some money by working in theatre, but for me, it's humiliating. And really, most plays don't even need it. Music to Ibsen, Wilde, or Molière... Forgive me, but music just fills in the time, so it will seem to pass faster. But it passes oh, so slowly, especially if the play's badly directed. Do you want to get a drink somewhere while we're out?

FIRST
Aren't you talkative today? What's wrong with you? Are you ill? You don't want to compose it, all right, then, don't compose it, but don't make it a bigger deal than it is.

SECOND
I'm not making a big deal out of it. I'm serious. If you insist on having music in the play, I can give you something that I've already done, but no way will I be staying up all night composing anything new.

FIRST
You are making a big deal out of it. You see, you work in isolation. All you have to do is spread out the notes on a piece of paper, and that's it – a happy-go-lucky artist. And me? I have to deal with dozens of people on daily basis. Even an actor who just brings in the tray needs to have it all explained: why is he bringing that damned tray, and what does him bringing it mean for the play. I have to explain to the carpenter the philosophical underpinnings of the playwright's intentions. Otherwise, he can end up making such furniture that people will be rolling in the aisles with laughter. I've lived through stories like that; trust me, I've seen it all. They say, oh, a young, inexperienced director, but do they know what I went through?

SECOND
We're all working on overdrive. For the holiest of our ideas, or our careers – which might as well be one and the same.

FIRST
What do you mean 'one and the same'? It's either this or that. I'm always burning up idealistically. I want to make good theatre. Every time and everywhere. Let's go. Or wait, you go by yourself, and let's meet at the coffee house in half an hour.

SECOND
Good b... *(Cuts it.)*

FIRST
(Alone on stage, shuffles through his papers and various items hidden in his suitcase.) I need to organize this suitcase. I need to do that by myself and I don't have the time.

THIRD
I'm not making a happening! That is, I am making a happening, but differently. I'm making theatre. I take a group of people – the photographer; former prompter; Waldo, the painter; you know all of them – and I'm making theatre. Intellectual, and fuck, yes, metaphysical theatre. I have a couple of ideas, directorial ideas.
They're just too good to pass up. I don't feel like painting anymore, what am I supposed to paint?

FIRST
Paintings.

THIRD
What paintings? No. Theatre. I feel I have a gift! You have the education, you've been trained and all that, but I, I have a gift. In my theatre, there won't be any decorations, no sets. What for? Actors are decorative enough.

FIRST
What actors? Where are you gonna get those actors from?

THIRD
My actors, fifteen of them, that's enough, I have them. Oh, how I'll be envied! Nothing like that has ever been done before.

FIRST
And isn't done yet.

THIRD
What 'isn't done yet'? It's done already. We signed a
contract for three tours. I don't know yet what I'll do,
but it will be marvelous, nothing short of marvelous.
They do adaptations of everything these days: Kafka, no,
not Kafka, poetry, prose, drama, everything. I'll do an
adaptation of horoscopes. Get it? Nobody will be allowed
to leave the theatre until his sign, be it Aries or Taurus,
appears to him.

FIRST
What Aries or Taurus?

THIRD
(Looking at him with condescension.) Bro, use your brain, if
you have it… Horoscopes, Pisces, Gemini, and all that.
Plus, Witkacy and his Countesses. And perverts. Big art
and small men. Contrast! Everything for real, but really,
only make-believe. Let them sweat, trying to figure it out.

FIRST
Who's going to sweat?

THIRD
The audience, of course, and the critics, who else? Oh,
they'll sweat trying to figure out with their little brains
what it's all about. We'll have a blast. Like in a circus,
we'll be juggling them back and forth.

FIRST
(Laughing.) But the prompter limps. How is he supposed
to juggle?

THIRD
(Sarcastically.) You really are a good audience, you know?
You never get anything even if it stares you right in your

face! The director has to a) anticipate, b) understand, c) know. Otherwise, he can just kiss his directing career goodbye.

FIRST
And start painting!

THIRD
No, to paint you have to know how, everyone knows that. *A propos*, Ionesco is a has-been, right? What do you think?

FIRST
No, not at all.

THIRD
But the Swiss are? Frish, Dürrenmatt – what's up with that? *(Mocking.)* Swiss are still important, but only as guards for the Pope. So, what's 'in' right now? In Paris, nothing, nada, zip. I saw a couple of things while I was there. Unbearable. Everyone's over, done. But, the actors are good – *(Correcting himself.)* – some of them. I'll start with Gemini, twins, May and June. Twins, you see, they're double. They are so talented, but lazy. Waldo, the painter, he'll do a good job too; he's also lazy. The world is doubled, divided, fucked up, just like the twins. *(Forcefully.)* And contrasts: the Countess peels a turnip, sitting together with a simple weaver – or even better – with a cleaning lady. They both have the same problems. The world integrated but divided, you got that?

FIRST
So what?

THIRD
(Discouraged.) So what? You don't get it, don't you? Maybe I should just do a simple, basic happening? *(Perks up.)* No, theatre. It has to be *theatre*. In my theatre, the main part will belong to the underpants. Every actor wearing underpants in a different color. They'll be easy to differentiate. They can take them off and put them on, exchanging them amongst themselves.

FIRST
After the soccer match, the soccer players exchange their
sweaty T-shirts.

THIRD
Underpants are better. I know what I'm talking about.
Sure, they can be sweaty, what's that to me. That's not
what it's all about.

FIRST
And what is it all about?

THIRD
You don't get it. Maybe it's even better. I'm not literal.
Any hillbilly can do that, be literal. I've always told you:
don't do anything literal. Art with a thesis, with a key!
Key! Keys are at the porter, as the prompter says. In my
theatre, he'll be the first actor to speak.

FIRST
Who? Porter?

THIRD
No, the prompter. He's prompted me with that idea of the
underpants.

FIRST
Clear enough. He's a prompter so he prompts.

THIRD
Wait a minute. You know what? That woman who was
interviewing you the other day – I'll take her too. She'll
be good. And she wants it badly, oh she wants it. She
already agreed to it.

FIRST
Her? On stage? Are you kidding me? She's like dead
wood. But whatever, it's your show...

THIRD
There'll be no stage in my theatre. Actors will be mixed
up with the audience. Audience members don't have to be

paid because, well, it's the audience that pays. And actors, they want to act anyways, so I'll pay them something, but just a little bit…

FIRST
Real art has never made any profit. Real greatness costs money, as one basketball player used to say. Can you just imagine how much he had to pay for his suit! Just the fabric alone – four, five yards – and without the vest too.

THIRD
I don't want any basketball players. They'd steal all the attention.

FIRST
There was this gang of shoplifters in England. Bunch of midgets *(Gestures.)* would come into the store with one six-footer. While the big guy was making faces, drawing everyone's attention, the midgets took whatever they wanted, unnoticed. They were in business for six years, eventually growing up to be respectable citizens, bowler hats and all that.

THIRD
(Pensive, but lucid.) If they were midgets, how could have they grown up? You know what, I have an idea. I'll bring in a couple of naked women. Shock! Here's everyone dressed, and there they come in, naked, with big boobs, fake smiles. Complete stunner, but still, the world divided…

FIRST
The one who interviewed you won't get naked. She wants to act in a theatre, you know. She told me so herself. She's a piece of wood, but wants to act nonetheless.

THIRD
So? I'll take someone else. *(Articulating disgust.)* Nema problema – as the Croats say.

FIRST
Or, as the illegal Turks say, nix problem. They're more Western-like, I guess.

THIRD
Whatever. You get it.

FIRST
(Jokingly.) About those naked women – what do you need them for? There's plenty of them nowadays in every movie. That's not how you make real theatre.

THIRD
You won't discourage me. No way! I know that I want.

FIRST
What I want. Determiner.

THIRD
What? What determiner?

FIRST
Determiner!

THIRD
Ah, determiner! I get it.

FIRST
What do you get?

THIRD
Wait a minute, what do you mean? Determiner, what?

FIRST
(Explains calmly, like a teacher.) A determiner is a form of speech, an interrogative pronoun. Its compound is formed with the suffix 'ever.' It can also be used as an interrogative adjective.

THIRD
Are you sure? Did you read all this somewhere? *(Pause.)* You know what happened to me the other day? I'm walking, straight ahead *(Slower.)* straight ahead, and here I run into...

FIRST
A pile of mud.

THIRD
(Turning his head.) No. I run into an acquaintance. I haven't seen him in twenty years. Well, maybe twelve, but still...

FIRST
Hold on. I don't get it.

THIRD
He has been coming to see my happenings, to see how they're done. But when I was making my happenings, I wasn't looking at him, or for him, because he was just one of many other people out there.

FIRST
(Slowly.) So, you don't want my help?

THIRD
I'm the best person to handle my own ideas. Maybe I'll call you later, some other time. *(Pause.)* Are you in a hurry?

FIRST
Yes, I have an important meeting. I need to take time to prepare for it.

THIRD
Oh, OK. Understood. *(Both exit in different directions.)*

II MENUET

SECOND

(Alone.) Isolation and indifference – that's what plagues us. How will my poor, worn-out brain handle all that? At some point, people began to believe that there is nothing easier than to live. Just like that, you live and all's good. Only those who **want** to have problems have them. But that's not how it works. Sooner or later life will catch up with you, punch you in the face, and dump you in a pile of mud. And as you're lying there in the puddle of dirt, you'll wonder, what am I doing here in all this dirt? After all, my shoes were clean and my hands were too – they were always clean. And now, I'm covered in mud and dirt...

THIRD

(Entering, seems giddy for some reason, but not in good shape.) You look like crap today. What's this about? Didn't get any sleep last night? Heh? Or something else... *(Yawning.)* ... rinking...iness...esome...*(Yawning.)* I'm really surprised. Why are you doing all that? As far as I'm concerned, I just **don't** have the energy. If you **want** to know...

SECOND

I don't want to know. If you only knew how little energy I have sometimes.

THIRD

(Dismissive.) There are more people like ourselves, you know. We could form the First International. The masses will be behind us... The ideals in front of us. Let's go!

SECOND

(Pensive.) Go – where? *(To himself.)* Life's like one grotesque dream. You know what one philosopher said?

THIRD

Which one? The one with the beard? What does he know? Wife cheats on him, and he's lecturing everyone about the superiority of ideals over the material life. He's a fanatic, though a well-read one.

SECOND

She doesn't cheat on him. She's sleeping around, and
then, she tells him all about it. They want to have a
marriage like Sartre's. Equal access, etc., such nonsense:
we're together, but getting what we want on the side. Such
an existential fad. That dumb cow of Sartre's is crazy, I'm
telling you. She writes everything down. If she'd actually
enjoyed everything she's doing, she would have kept it to
herself, content with her sex appeal and popularity, but
no, that dumb cow analyzes everything, and she gets paid
to do it too.

THIRD

Money well earned. Unlike you, quick show, quick cash.
Do you believe in an afterlife? Or do you think this life
is all we've got? Don't look ahead, just get ahead. But
I'm not so sure... Do they have dumplings / pierogi / up
there that taste like the ones my aunt makes? My mouth
waters just thinking about them! As a matter of fact, she
doesn't even use that much cheese, but still, what a taste!
Eventually, you become obsessed: all you can think of
are her dumplings. The dumplings become your one sole
reason for living, your *raison d'être*!

SECOND

But I don't like dumplings, unless they're stuffed with
meat. But even then, they're so-so.

THIRD

They're better when they're stuffed with cheese. But you
need to add pepper. *(Pause.)* And now, a few sit-ups.
(Does a few sit-ups.) So, what I hear you saying is that this
Sartre woman is a common whore? And I was under the
impression...

SECOND

Yes, right, you were under the impression.

THIRD

(Quietly.) Why don't you tell me, in confidence, why

peppered dumplings are so good and peppered life not so much?

SECOND
Oh, your aphorisms...

THIRD
Nobody understands them. Like my art – only a few get it.

SECOND
Art has to be hard to get. The harder to get it is, the better it is.

THIRD
That's the case with 'Fragments.' I like those parts that I don't quite understand. *(Seriously.)* There are a few great thoughts in there; some are even deep. And form! What an idea to have a dialogue made up of names, from A to Z. This way, even the biggest idiot will finally catch what's going on. He can even predict an ending!

SECOND
Heidegger wrote quite a lot about ending, how predictable it is. In life, anything can happen, but nothing is certain. Only death is certain.

THIRD
You oversimplify that, but generally, you're right. That's what Heidegger wrote. You know, your simplification has all the qualities of a great aphorism.

SECOND
No need to suck up to me. I said that sentence six hundred times already – sixhundred times, as our friend would say.

THIRD
Do we have to talk about him behind his back?

SECOND
When will he finally show up? Big director and he comes in late.

THIRD
He comes late.

SECOND
Whatever. That's how **he** says it. I'm **hung** up – he says. Whatever; he can talk however he wants if only he would show up already. This way, we'll never finish it. And what's going to happen with all of the separate rehearsals with the cello player?

FIRST
(Entering, happy, energetic, smiling and somewhat radiant and inspired.) Let's get to work! To work!

SECOND
Good morning. That's what you should start with.

FIRST
(Looking at the SECOND.) Good morning. You always try to nip me a little, always, right from the start. You don't like me, don't you?

THIRD
Let's forget about likes and dislikes. Let's get to work!

FIRST
That's what I just said: let's get to work! *(Perking up.)* This scene should be played much zazzier! It's not just a dialogue. It's a grand, passionate, obsessive fight over principles.

THIRD
Where do you see any principles? It's pure nonsense. But since it's written by an intelligent writer, everyone swoons.

SECOND
I think...

FIRST
Your job is to act well, not to think.

SECOND
I beg your pardon, but I'm allowed to think. This is a free country – maybe you've missed that – so I think if I want to.

FIRST
Just act, don't think. But well, act well – don't butcher it.

SECOND
(Calmly.) I think that the text itself is smart, but its author not so much. It happens quite often that the play outgrows its author. It surprises us, oh, just like that, we gape in surprise. *(Widens his eyes in surprise.)*

FIRST
What do we do? I don't get it. Please, can you focus and play that scene again – just like the last time, but differently. Is that clear?

THIRD
No.

FIRST
Unclear?

THIRD
Clear.

FIRST
So it's clear!

THIRD
Unclear.

FIRST
You just said it yourself that it's clear.

THIRD
I said it is clear that it's unclear because you asked if it's unclear. So I replied, instinctively and correctly, may I add, that it's clear, thinking that it's clear that it's unclear.

FIRST
You confuse me. Focus, and do what I say – act, just the way you did it last time, but this time, do it differently. *(To both.)* Is that clear?

SECOND
(Eagerly.) Clear.

FIRST
(To THIRD.) You see, that's the way to do it!

THIRD
(Offended.) To do what? To suck up to you, that's what you want? Then, you'll have a comfortable working environment? I care about art, with a capital A – Art. Or at least, a bigger A, a medium A.

SECOND
(Getting in the middle between FIRST and THIRD.) There is no medium A. It's either small or large A, like small and large beer.

FIRST
(To SECOND.) You know, I'll tell you something. *(Pause.)* Or, maybe not. Better yet, let's go over the Heidegger scene again.

THIRD
It's all same to me. You want the Heidegger scene, fine.

FIRST
(Furious.) I don't understand it. What do you mean, 'It's all the same to me'? Do you know what you're saying? It's

all the same to you who is in power? Idiot, genius, angel, beast – all the same? Yes?

SECOND
(Again, getting in the middle of their argument.) When we say, 'it's all the same,' what we usually mean is that we don't think we have any say about what's going on or what's going to happen. For example, I have no say about who will become the artistic director of the operetta in our town, or who will become the dean of the medical school in Olsztyn. That's an appropriate occasion to say it: it's all the same to me.

FIRST
Do you know anyone from Olsztyn? It's a very nice town. And the medical school releases some very good doctors; that's what I've heard, at least.

SECOND
The school produces good doctors, but they end up being bad.

FIRST
Explain, please.

SECOND
(To THIRD.) Did you get it?

THIRD
Yes, I did.

SECOND
(To FIRST.) You see.

FIRST
I don't see anything. Let's rehearse.

THIRD
(Acting, from 'Fragment'.) Nicholas, I've read Heidegger's *Metaphysics* and I didn't understand a word of it.

SECOND
Did you read it carefully?

THIRD
Yes, but regardless, I didn't understand it.

FIRST
(Interrupting them.) Wrong! Wrong! It's all wrong! That is, it's all good – but all wrong. *(To THIRD.)* You have to make it understood that you didn't understand a word. Do you understand?

THIRD
I understand.

FIRST
What do you understand? *(Pause.)* One more time, let's go.

THIRD
Nicholas, I've read *Metaphysics*...

SECOND
Metaphysics...

FIRST
Why are you interrupting him?

SECOND
I'm correcting him. Metaphysics, not metaphysics. One should pronounce words correctly. That's what the author, culture and other such trivialities expect of us.

FIRST
(Ironically.) Really? That is how it should be pronounced? Are you sure?

SECOND
I'm sure.

THIRD
A cello solo comes in here, and we act over the music. Is it really important how to pronounce each word? The meaning is important.

SECOND
Hold on, hold on. *(Coming to a realization.)* The word came first.

THIRD
In the Bible, but not in real life. The first man, a half monkey, **already** mumbled some inarticulate sounds that already had some meanings, some content. *(Faster.)* Come here! Come here! Or, danger; or, lion, son of a bitch, get the hell out of here, run, run! Or, I got you, you monkey. Now, you're mine and I'll never let you go! And boom, boom, boom. And then, I sneak up on you again. *(Excited by his inventiveness.)* I hide behind the bushes, nasty like all monkeys, and boom, I hit a girlfriend on the head with an orange. She's screaming at me, while I hide again in the bushes...

FIRST
Why don't you get out of those bushes already and tell us what you want. It's supposed to be a rehearsal. What the hell are you doing?

THIRD
My point is that the content is more important than the form. Even without language, the first primitive men communicated something among themselves.

FIRST
Can you just say it in a normal, human way?

SECOND
I liked it. *(Mocking THIRD.)* Come here! Come here! And boom, boom, boom – and in the bushes, and orange in the head – very good!

FIRST
Let's get to work! One more time.

THIRD
What for? I know everything already. Why do we need to repeat the same texts over and over again. Most of the time we read them anyways, so what for?

FIRST
What for, what for! You have to work, work hard to
accomplish the essential, fundamental artistic result – you
have to work! So you think, I wouldn't prefer to sit in a
nice office, pushing papers, once a week push them a bit
harder, and be all set for the rest of my life. Grow roses in
the backyard and tell bullshit stories to my grandchildren.
And what happens to a director? When he gets old, they'll
say 'he's finished.' Someone else will add: 'he always only
pretended to be a great artist.' The newspapers will point
out that he hasn't directed anything interesting in a long
while. Ruin and zero. Sodom and Gomorrah. You can't
even hang yourself because you're too weak and too old...
and what...

Silence. Nobody says anything. Long pause.

SECOND
This is what they call an awkward silence. Nobody has
anything to say. Why don't we all sing something together.

THIRD
In choir or in unison?

SECOND
Both.

FIRST
I'm not going to sing.

FIRST
Someone has to sing.

THIRD
"I don't sing, so someone else could." Shakespeare.

FIRST
No, that's not how it goes. One person sings and another
one doesn't – and that's how it is. That's how it should be.

THIRD
I don't have to sing. I can dance. *(Dances without music,
mumbling to himself and marking the rhythms.)*

SECOND
(*Looks at him attentively*. THIRD *starts dancing like Fred Astaire*.) I've seen that dance somewhere. In a movie.

THIRD
I've never danced in a movie.

SECOND
I know why you'd say so. (*Grows pensive, while THIRD continues to dance*.) You're not very original.

THIRD
(*Dancing.*) The uniqueness of the dance doesn't depend on its originality, but on synchronization. (*Showing.*) The music and movement needs to be synchronized. And in my dance, they are.

SECOND
They are indeed, but it's not original. The tango, that's original. (*Sings loudly, swaying to the rhythm of the song.*)

FIRST
Gentlemen, gentlemen, please, be quiet. The neighbors. There is a meeting downstairs. They need to concentrate. They're morons, but decided to call a meeting, a scientific meeting...

SECOND
It doesn't bother me. They can concentrate all they want. The tango is original!

FIRST
(*Expertly.*) The waltz is original. The tango is Argentine. From Peron's country. What a loathsome creep.

THIRD
Mazurka!

FIRST
What mazurka?

THIRD
Mazurka.

FIRST
Ah, mazurka. *(Pause.)* No, the waltz.

SECOND
The tango!

FIRST
Not at all. The waltz! *(The conversation turns into improvisation. It lasts for a while. They argue passionately, separate, and come together again. Suddenly, they step five steps forward and start dancing a polonaise in sync. The music starts. They face the audience like can-can girls.)*

SECOND
(Fixing his shoe.) It was a very expressive arrangement. Following Gombrowicz, our beloved, we began with a polonaise and ended with my Argentine tango. I don't want to hear from anyone that we've been manipulated, directed. It simply just happened.

THIRD
Let's get back to the text, to acting.

FIRST
To the text! To hell with dancing. It's so tiresome.

SECOND
(To the FIRST.) You know what, for many years now, I've been dreaming of getting a biiiiig part, so big that it would make everyone else look very small *(He makes a gesture.)*

FIRST
So small? *(Gestures.)*

SECOND
Yes, so small.

FIRST
Or maybe even smaller? *(Gestures again.)*

SECOND
No. *(Gestures.)* Only that small. I'd be happy with that.

FIRST
(Having an epiphany.) So then, you'd be better than them!

SECOND
Yes, then I'd be at peace.

FIRST
And the others? Would they be at peace **too**? What would they do to you...

SECOND
They would do nothing. What could they do? The big ones are untouchable.

FIRST
That's true, but envy...

SECOND
If you're big, what do you care!

(Silence, music.)

III ANDANTE

SECOND
Ha! *(Louder.)* Ha! *(Quieter.)* Ha! *(Very quiet.)* Ha! *(Waiting for the audience's reaction. Whatever it is, it doesn't matter.)* Not too long ago, someone was trying to tell me that nobody talks about me anymore. 'Nobody mentions you, nobody writes about you. And at one time, there was so much hoopla around everything you did. What happened?' – the guy asked, pretending to care. Time will tell, I tell him, and if they don't talk, it doesn't prove anything. I'll tell you in confidence, *(Loud whisper.)* it's not true! They talk, a lot! See, I've got the latest newspaper here, where – I'll read it to you. – I used to read to my grandfather. This newspaper has sixteen pages, a lot of ads and news... *(Reads.)*

In Schaeffer town, Bi Schaeffer, a gardener with a police record, broke into the bank safe and ate all of the sandwiches that were stored there by the Head Cashier of Schaeffer and Schaefferson. Then, taking advantage of the fact that the night guard, B. J. Schaeffer, was taking a beer nap, Bi Schaeffer left unnoticed, taking with him the money-counting machine made by Schaeffers and Schaeffers. Besides the sandwiches, about two hundred thirty thousand well-cooled dollars are also missing. The inspector Schaeffer, who heads the investigation, noted that the money is definitively gone. All that was left was the smell of the thief's sweater. Unfortunately, the local police dog, Schaefff, was not able to locate the owner of the fragrant sweater. Prosecutor B. B. Schaeffer postponed the case, stating on local TV that he has more important cases to worry about, like the highly publicized murder of the multimillionaire Schaeffer, who was killed when vacationing with his girlfriend and a few mystery novels at a nearby resort, Schaeffersville.

News from Lyon. The city mayor, Julien Schaeffer, turned his city into one huge casino, thereby singlehandedly saving the municipal budget and his own hard-earned reputation as a staunch catholic and communist. The first client of the biggest and – we can already say – the leading casino in Lyon, the Schaefferais, was the street singer and millionaire Jules Schaeffer, who has instantaneously gambled away his yearly earnings.

In Kostarica, the minister of finances, Juan Jose Schaeffer, from San Schaefferio, died of a laugh attack. As it appears, there was plenty of money in the national safe, probably deposited there by foreign intelligence. The Nigerian leader of the rebels, Mbwba Powabu Schaefferm, denies any connection to the money, which in itself is surprising since nobody was asking him about any connections.

Moscow. The Russian scientist Gaspadislaw Julianowich Schaeffer, who studies the genetics of fruit, and who works at the leading kolkhoz, Schaefferovo, created a new fruit, combining the fruit of brotherhood with the fruit of friendship. The local agronomist, Schaeffer Schaefferowich Schaeffchenko, praised the new fruit, calling it perfect.

Tokyo. An unknown man, quite possibly the well-known Sicilian Mafioso Michaelangelo Schaeffer (exactly, Schaefferini), smuggled from Japan the proverbial Japanese work ethic, while smuggling into Japan the famous Italian joviality and love of singing. Japanese Prime Minister Bogumitsu Schaefferamata (once known as the German spy Gottlieb Ephraim Schaeffer!) sang at the last meeting of the Japanese parliament, behaving very jovially, which was immediately interpreted as an American provocation.

In the Carpathian town of Lower Schaefferowo, on the celebrated Schaeffer Day, Mr. and Mr. Schaeffer welcomed twins. Right away, the boys decided to become composers. Now, to thirty-eight esteemed Polish composers spread all over the world, we can also add Boguslaw and Julian Schaeffer. Fortunately, they both are still babies. The gossip that the two boys can sit up is either untrue or a misinterpretation. The boys do sit but can't talk. The older one, Boguslaw, suffers from a strange phobia: he hates staff paper. He also hates eggs, which is understandable. Boguslaw's phobia is entered into the Guinness Schaeffer Book of Phobia Records in eight hundred fifteenth place, under the section "Art."

Netherlander tattoo artist Schaeffers van Schaeffer would like to apologize to one of his clients for tattooing an insufficiently sexy woman on his back. But it is all in vain. The client, as it happened, was the famous portrait artist Bory Ary Schaeffer, who went mad when he saw his back in the mirror. As expected, Bory Ary Schaeffer is currently being treated in the psychiatric ward of Dr. Schaeffer.

Western European journalists received from Schaeffer Books a handy lexicon of the life and work of Schaeffer. There is also a special Schaeffer infoline that's updated twice a day with new details about Schaeffer's life. Sam Schaeffer, in an interview with Samuel Yitzhak Schaeffer, said that he is not satisfied with the lexicon, as it doesn't have entries for "humility," "debts," "insomnia," and "a short-term attention span." The publisher, J. J. Schaeffer,

representing Schaeffers Publishing Company, assured
the composer that the next editions will include all of the
omissions. Regardless of those assurances, the composer
sued the editor, and it looks like he might win the lawsuit.
He might also win a large settlement, as he has hired
a well-known and respected New York lawyer, Boris
Schaeffer Jr., a son of the once-famous Mafia lawyer of the
1930s, Boris Schaeffer, Sr.

Enter FIRST.

FIRST
(Loud.) Ah! All you care about are newspapers! A!
"Schaeffer Time Magazine." My wife subscribes to it!
She claims we'll never have such a well-edited newspaper
ever again, if this one ever stops being published. Every
evening, she prays for the health of the editor in chief,
what's his name, Boom Schaeffer.

SECOND
The genius editor and brilliant publisher in one person.
You know what he printed in the last few issues? No? You
don't? *(Triumphantly.)* Schaeffer's last novel! In chapters,
but in reverse order, from the end to the beginning. He
wants the people to buy the book too when he releases it!
Genius, right? Paying twice for the same thing, backwards
and forwards. Isn't he a pure genius, or what?

FIRST
Yeeees.

SECOND
Backwards and forwards *(Pronounces it together
"backwardsandforwards".)*

THIRD
(Entering on the last words.) I don't understand what you're
saying! Are you learning a new language? Hold on, let me
guess. What language can it be? The native language of
the British Solomon Isles...

SECOND
Genius! *(To FIRST, ignoring the THIRD.)* And he prints
everything in this newspaper of his! Lately, he even
printed the reviews of Schaeffer's concerts, you know, that
one-eyed piano player. He hires the best critics. You can't
deny that bringing Bousku Mircea Schaefferusku from
Transylvania was a great idea! He's Romanian, in fact,
but how he writes! Like the French, or maybe even better
because he actually uses spell-check. He never makes any
errors. According to Schaeffer, the piano player – never!
You know what he recently wrote about you? The maestro
could close his second eye and no ear would ever notice it!

THIRD
Clever and funny too! Two chickens with one knife
(Joyously.) Swoosh!

FIRST
(Calmly.) Herder, not Schaeffer, but Johann Gottfried
Herder, philosopher and theologist, said once that there
are only two tyrants in the world: **accident** and **time**! It
is an accident that I have two actors who want to do
everything but act. And time, we don't have much of
it. *(Excited.)* To work! Let's start from the beginning,
from the very first scene. Nothing is happening, tension,
cello player plays for a while now, the two actors start
talking. In your version, it sounds rather weak. *(Mocking
them.)* 'Lanzylm... What, Lapolinary? Nothing, nothing.
You wanted to say someth'?' I can't listen to it calmly.
No tension, no secret! It should be performed like a
mysterium tremendum. Say: 'Anzelm...' – quietly, but
with passion, grippingly, unraveling a new world of
interrelations that connect people. Let's think! Why does
Apollinaire open his mouth at all? Why isn't he just quiet
as if he were mute, why isn't he just listening to the music,
or fixing his pants... Why?

THIRD
Right, why?

FIRST
I'm asking you.

THIRD
Why are you asking and don't answer yourself. If you know the answer, then tell it!

FIRST
He opens his mouth because he can't be silent.

SECOND
Anzelm…

THIRD
What, Apollinaire?

SECOND
Nothing, nothing. *(And so on. Short improvisation not connected with either "Fragment" or with anything else that they've already talked about. After a while, the SECOND's voice can be heard.)* I think I need to eat something right now. *(He talks, while the other two watch him.)* One guy came to a very nice restaurant with his own food and he started preparing his own meal. When he was whipping an egg to make a mayonnaise, the waiter approached him, asking him to leave. So, he responds that food in restaurants has never been good – he even quoted from Gide and Schaeffer's diaries – and that he likes to prepare everything himself. Finally, they threw him out of the restaurant, and when he was out, he was still explaining that he didn't mean to offend anyone, not the chef or the wait staff, that 'naturalia sunt fecalia' and so on… *(All three start talking about various issues connected to the story, but also about other things **not** connected to the story. They exit, and their voices slowly fade away.)*

IV FINALE

FIRST
Do you know where our beloved colleague might be? We're always waiting for him. Punctuality is not one of

his virtues. Does he have any virtues at all, besides being overly confident? *(Pause.)* Do you know where he could be right now?

SECOND
I don't.

FIRST
(Pensive.) You don't know. What *do* we know in general. Very little. *(Perking up.)* Take me, for example. I've got no idea what Chopin looked like. In one daguerreotype photograph, he looks at us, somber, seriously ill, as if he were saying: 'Just look, look, what a life I have. Screwed up.' And then, he died. The photographer took such a detailed photo as if he wanted to capture something special. In fact, you could stare at this photograph for hours. I did that once. Eventually, you get to know his face pretty well, but you still don't know anything about him.

SECOND
And what would you want to know?

FIRST
How was his life?

SECOND
With George Sand? Who knows – she was writing all the time. She had a compulsion to write novels. The public read them all, and **she** wrote them because they read them. They read them because **she** wrote them. Circulus vitiosus – vicious circle. It's a common occurrence whenever art's concerned.

FIRST
No! How was his life in **general**. We know him casually, what he looks like, his habits, but you see – it's not the total knowledge about a man's life. I want to know how he was doing in life.

SECOND
How are you doing in life? If I were to ask you...?

FIRST
(Makes wry face.) Eh, normally…

SECOND
Just like him. Except, he wouldn't make faces like that.
(Makes a face.) He was honest, and that's why he had a lot
of friends.

FIRST
(Discontented.) What are you saying! *(Surprised.)* So,
according to you, it's enough to be honest to have
a friend? Let me be honest with you then. You're a
schmuck, not an actor! A slightly more complex text, and
you drool and spit. Even those who sit in the twentieth
row can see it. Your zipper is open quite often, and you're
a number one gossip monger. *(Pause.)* So what? Are
we friends yet? I am so happy – really – I am so happy.
(Attempts to embrace the SECOND.)

SECOND
(Escaping with disgust.) Let me zip my pants. – It's a total
libel. The shirt – maybe, I agree, I sometimes forget to
button it up, but the pants – never. You must've mixed me
up with someone else.

FIRST
There's no mix-up. **You** are wearing **your** pants. What
nonsense are you suggesting? It's you, I'm telling you.
And gossiping – oh, yes you do gossip; even right now
you claim I'm taking you for someone else. It's disgusting.
I can only imagine what you're saying behind *my* back!

SECOND
Why do you think someone's talking about you behind
your back? Nobody has been talking about you for a
long time. 'He's finished, zero' – that's all that they're
saying and only casually, in passing, at some academic
conference!

FIRST
(Calmly.) You're putting on airs, but be careful, the

ceilings are pretty low here *(Shows that one can hit one's head if not careful.)* – what do you need that for. . . .

SECOND
(Looks absentmindedly, detached.) Sometimes I have a dream that I go up and up, flying, waving my arms like Daedalus, only calmly. The people are looking up at me. I can sense their gaze, their admiration, but I don't pay any attention. I just fly, fly . . .

THIRD
(Entering on the last word. Stops.) Which way are you flying? West?

SECOND
(Earnestly dreamy.) No. It's a beautiful day. I fly just like that, with no direction. I cast a large shadow on the fields and hills. Sometimes, I lower myself a bit, but then, I still know that if I only wanted to I could go up at any moment. The higher up I am, the warmer, brighter it gets . . . Sometimes, someone approaches me, but I can just see the clumsy s.o.b. he is, how tired he is. He'll surely land on his stomach any minute now. But not me. I fly and fly, effortlessly. I'm humble, so I don't think I'm better than him, but maybe I am better. Sometimes I do think about that, but I tell myself, it's surely just a question of personality. Someone else can't do it, but I can.

FIRST
(Loudly, sharp.) What can you do?

SECOND
(Suddenly, as if awaken from a dream.) What? What time is it?

FIRST
(To the THIRD, ignoring the SECOND.) We've been talking about Chopin. In this photo, for example, he looks like he's got tuberculosis. He spent his days writing music – and what music!

THIRD
I thought we were talking about flying.

FIRST
What flying? What? No. We've been talking about
Chopin: what kind of life he had.

THIRD
Cool! *(Pause.)* He didn't live in our times.

FIRST
If he did, he would have been cured. Everyone gets cured
of tuberculosis nowadays, like they do of friendship.

SECOND
(Still a bit dreamy, but awake.) Friendship. You dare to
speak of friendship. You libel me in my face and you dare
to talk about friendship. *(To THIRD.)* Do you know what he
said?

THIRD
I'm sorry, but I'd rather not get mixed up in someone
else's business, even if it's an important business, as I'm
sure yours is. I have lost a number of good friends this
way.

FIRST
Do you see any friends here? You want to say something,
say it. But be honest. I'm not afraid to hear anything you
can throw at me. I'm clean as a tear.

THIRD
And we're dirty? What are you suggesting?

FIRST
You're always late! One could fix a broken clock waiting
for you.

THIRD
You don't say? *(Pause.)* Do you know why I'm always
late, as you distastefully pointed out? *(Louder.)* Because I
have a thousand other things to do besides this meeting.

And you don't. And that's the main difference between us. *(Excited, getting furious.)* A big difference, if you must know.

SECOND
(Mockingly, making references to the previous scene which he remembered. His entire statement is clearly aimed at the FIRST. THIRD listens to him, ignoring the FIRST.) Lanzylmje! What's up did he buy it? He wasn't scared?

THIRD
(Ignoring the FIRST, who like an 'idiot' listens attentively to their conversation.) Why should he be scared, Lapolinary? I'm a walking guarantee. After all, he can at any minute...

SECOND
Yes, yes, but you know how he can be. All's good and dandy, until it isn't, and bam! He serves you a shitload of crap.

THIRD
Not this time. This time, I served *him*.

SECOND
Shit? Cute little shit?

THIRD
(Very content.) With a guarantee! Shit-eater!

FIRST doesn't understand anything. SECOND and THIRD talk to each other, ignoring the FIRST. They put their hands on him, as if he were a statue. They are completely engrossed in their conversation, which could emanate all kinds of emotions, affects and laughter. They know their language very well. They have no problem understanding and expressing themselves.

SECOND
It's easy to bend on the bench!

THIRD
(Intimately.) He begs for bribe, bastard, and bum.

SECOND
(He speaks looking at the audience, as if he didn't understand a thing of what he's saying.) Husband hunter, but lives like cohabitanter.

THIRD
Biece of bake! Beautified bitch was on the beach, buying and selling it cheap!

SECOND
(With condescension.) Bungry beggar beasy bought buddles!

THIRD
The boom of bastard bribes breaks every battered bum!

SECOND
The bitch will finally break the bastard!

THIRD
Bah, don't be a dirtbag!

SECOND
He can beg and beg, but he'll be busted!

THIRD
(As if he were saying: 'What a nice guy and completely gone crazy'.) Berated, berated, but behind bushes he bought borrowed time, the brilliant bogus bastard!

SECOND
And how easy breezy, the benefactor!

THIRD
And how benevolent! Easily burnable! Bat, bat, but still a brat!

SECOND
Break, but without making it a big brawl. But, no, he brings a big bag of billion bucks. Bastard!

THIRD
Bastardy bastard! What a bird!

SECOND
Here, he begs; and here, such a bluff.

THIRD
The shit burns bright red!

SECOND
You should say: burns brightly. Kitchen-sink Latin can get
your brain flattened.

THIRD
And how it has gotten?

SECOND
(About FIRST.) Just look, he lost confidence all of a
sudden.

Long pause

FIRST
(Moving away.) Gentlemen, allow me to have a different
opinion.

SECOND
Have a different opinion. *(Ironically.)* You can have as
many of them as you want, even ten. A few disposable
ones, just in case. If you run out of them, you always have
extra replacements... *(Halts.)*

*FIRST and SECOND look at each other ominously. Long pause,
suddenly...*

FIRST
(Slowly, calmly approaches the THIRD.) Skinned of all will, I,
a metaphysical kangaroo with a pouch full of empty ideas,
what am I do to?

THIRD
(Calmly and also very seriously.) You have to be reborn. You
can't just remain intellectually drained.

FIRST
Sir! The rotten mattress of my brain won't accommodate any risky frisky moves any more.

THIRD
(Seriously.) So, you want to become a grand inquisitor of small dealings. You – the noble, open, so perfect, so set in your ways! *(Servile.)* Small backstabbings, treasons, and violence?

FIRST
I can't do anything. I have no will.

THIRD
You want to remain dead, an empty shell?

FIRST
I'm a simple guy, though so complicated a man.

Good in school, bad in deeds,

No greatness for me, just to be

Faithful to my wife,

My poor, poor life.

Though socially adept,

Void of will and depth.

He continues in prose, but it should be felt that he doesn't want to let go of poetry, that he will want to speak in verse whenever he can.

Just so you know, I hate calculated verbal refinement. Everything has to spring out of the **shock of the moment**. *(Earnest)* Oh, moment! Stay, last forever! *(Pathetic, madly.)* Oh God, how I suffer!

SECOND – with pity on his face – approaches the FIRST, wanting to help him as if he were disabled or mentally challenged, but the FIRST pushes him away.

FIRST

I feel like all the forces of the universe are gathered within me. I know what will happen with the world! The world won't disappear. It will last forever. The people will disappear, but what do I need them for? I am lonely anyways. *(Pathetically.)* My heart is still bleeding, can't you see it?! I am alone, but I need theatre because without it, who will see my loneliness! So, look, *(To the audience.)* here I am! *(Falling on his knees with a thud, tears his shirt; terrible pathos.)* I'm faithful to myself and my ideals, and you all *(Addressing nonexistent masses on the stage.)* – follow **me**!

Follow me, follow me
I'll show you the future,
I won't rest until I erase
All the dirt from the nation that for no reason
Bathes in shit. Oh, how I quiver, how I pant!

He does quiver and pant – reaching the height of the Romantic tension in imaginary theatre. How he does it, I don't know, but he does so for certain!

I swear, on the crime and holiness of my mother
For revolution you need blood and murder!
Fire the battleships! Open the barricades!
Leave your soccer games behind you, my brethen!
I'll show you the goal, the violence needs to be crushed,
How othcrwise will you get to heaven?
What will come out of you, oh, backward unwashed
Youth fattened on beer? It's a dangerous game you're playing!
Sooner or later, they'll turn you into capons. I'm telling
You this, I, the gentile.
I foresee you'll waste your lives,
If you don't go fight in the war
Screaming bravely: "Freedom or death!"
Our spirit has already sunk to the lower depths!

Pants and wheezes, falling to the ground with thud.

SECOND
(Skeptically.) All's well but you should say "sank" not
"sunk."

FIRST
You interrupted my soliloquy! You interrupted my
moment... *(Out of breath.)* Text can be corrected! Details
are not important. It's the idea that counts! Idea!

SECOND
Form counts too, sir, form counts too! And correct
pronunciation also counts!

FIRST
*(Very tired, only now emerging from the state which could be
called shock.)* What, what are you saying? *(Holding on to the
chair or something else, whimpering horrified.)* It could be a
heart attack.

THIRD
Less drinking, my dear, that's my advice, less vodka, and
you won't have a heart attack.

SECOND
And don't get drunk so often on Romantic pathos either!
You need to be in good shape to handle things like that,
as my friend, a plebeian kind of fellow, used to say.

THIRD
(Cheerfully.) Strong vodka, strong body!

SECOND
Jokes aside, my dear, the actor's dying here.

THIRD
Excited with passion, he was terrifying,
but look at him now, whimpering, sad and petrified...

SECOND
(Hitting the Romantic tone.)

...the light in his eyes is all gone,
Oh, how fearful, how forlorn.

THIRD
He should go quickly for 'observation'
So they can diagnose his mental constellation,
And tell him what is true and what is a delusion,
Though his mad craft enriches our own conclusion.

SECOND
Do you conclude that the medics can crack
The mystery of why the artist dies of a heart attack?
Treat your own heartaches, you dumb quacks,
Spitting clichés as if they were facts
That smokin', vodka and women
Are not good for artists, all are a bad omen.

THIRD
(Pause.) It's a good rhyme: women – omen. But you need
to work a bit harder on this. You can't just yap about
anything that comes into your head. You criticize doctors,
very well. But a little ache and pain here and there, and
you run to see your doctor as fast as you can. You're
the kind that always finds something mean to say about
everybody.

SECOND
Did I offend you with something? I apologize, I didn't
mean to. (To FIRST.) Are you feeling better?

FIRST
No, I'm faint and thirsty. Drink, I need a drink.

SECOND
But you've heard what I've just said: vodka, cigarettes –
they're not good for you. The world's greatest doctors will
tell you that.

FIRST
(Staring blankly at the SECOND.) What are they saying?
(Sadly.) Follow me, follow me. I'll show you the future, I
won't rest until I erase all the dirt from the nation... – No,
I can't. I'll never again act this scene so well...

THIRD
(As if he were talking to an idiot.) Don't worry. We have such problems here sometimes that yours don't even compare. Crying...

FIRST
(Repeating.) ...crying, crying...

SECOND
No need to. I can imagine **how** you act out crying. *(Pretends to cry for a brief moment.)*

THIRD
But he doesn't want to act it out. He wants to cry for real.

FIRST
(Long pause. Gets up quickly.) OK, gentlemen, let's go back to work. Enough with the chit-chat. Let's go back to the part with Heidegger. So, softly but expressively. More meat, less tripe.

THIRD
Good. More meat, less tripe. Meat – fried, boiled or grilled? And sauce, what kind of sauce?

FIRST
Joker, you are, aren't you? How are we going to play that "Fragment"? What will he say if he sees it and realizes that it's all shit and not "Fragment"? What are we gonna do then? When he forbids us from playing it? He'll just say casually: 'no.' I heard him say 'no' once, and I wouldn't want to hear it again. It's very unpleasant.

THIRD
Why do you give us such comparisons: meat, tripe, what's that for? It's not even in the script.

FIRST
And the director, my dear, is he in the script? You see, you always like to make things easy for yourself. Wham, bam, thank you ma'm. It's about art, real art, with a capital

(Looks at the SECOND and doesn't say "A," just repeats.)…real art, if you let me.

THIRD
Sure, I'll let you.

FIRST
Thank you.

THIRD
What for?

FIRST
What for? What for do you take me?

THIRD
For a man who is not easy to throw off his game. Balance you've got, I have to give it to you. You stand firm on both of your legs, and I like it, I like it a lot.

SECOND
(Impatiently.) So what? Are we trying this or not?

FIRST
We're trying. In fact, we're – as if – doing it right now.

THIRD
(Acting.) Waldo…

SECOND
What Wilhelm?

THIRD
Nothing, nothing, never mind. *(To FIRST.)* Here, your shirt got unbuttoned.

FIRST
(Ignoring him.) Your 'Nothing, nothing' ain't too deep. It can't be done like that.

THIRD
It can.

FIRST
It can't. Certainly it can't.

THIRD
It can. If I'm doing it, and without much effort, it means
that it can.

FIRST
You misunderstand me.

SECOND
Hold on, maybe I can explain it.

FIRST
It's my role to explain. *(To SECOND.)* Aha, what text do you
have?

SECOND
'What Wilhelm'

FIRST
You can't just drop it like that. In this line, 'What
Wilhelm,' there has to be desperation and tenderness in
that line.

SECOND
I'm not a faggot. Tenderness is inappropriate here.

FIRST
That's not what I meant. I meant, softness, sentiment.

SECOND
I'm not very sentimental, if you have to know.

FIRST
(Argumentatively.) But you're not saying it as yourself, but
as your character.

THIRD
He's always doing it 'as,' cuz he's a big ass himself.

FIRST
(To THIRD.) Stop right there. We'll have plenty of time to

argue, but right now, let's act. You say: Waldo – and there should be anxiety in your voice, existential tragism, the rottenness of the world, etc.

THIRD
What if it went perversely like that: Wal – Do. What? Like our genius actor used to say D-evil. He said it in the way that gave you goosebumps.

FIRST
So you think that if you say it, Wal-Do, you'll make the same impression? I doubt that.

THIRD
(Humbly.) Let me try.

FIRST
(Ignoring him.) There has to be anxiety in your voice.

THIRD
Or maybe like that: Wawl-dow! More stretched out, but it works here. Doesn't it?

SECOND
I would say it like 'Wal-doo' – quietly, calmly and anxiously.

FIRST
(Decisively.) No. Say it normally, like a normal human being, a normal simple human being.

THIRD
Waldo, fuck, listen to what I'm about to tell you...

SECOND
Mr. W, boss, I need to tell you something...

THIRD
Waldy, buddy, let me tell you something...

SECOND
Wally, com'over 'ere... *(With vulgar gesture.)*

FIRST
(Pensive, distant. He didn't participate in the last exchange.)
Art cannot be a reflection of one's prejudices, even those
about social class. The world will remain a mystery to us,
forever inscrutable. Cosmopolitan slavery of the soul *(To
the FIRST.)* – that's what we should be the most afraid of...

THIRD
(Continuing.) Walllek, let's go in pair...

SECOND
I feel something in the air.
You, Wally, hide your face
Or face a great disgrace.

THIRD
Beware of the street fight...

SECOND
Walde! Don't be such a smart ass...

FIRST
(Pensive.) Ach, to be back to the world of rococo...
Illusions in the theatre, but what illusions were
they! Permanent masquerade, with so much spirit.
Someone called this period an epoch of theatocracy...
Theatres everywhere: at the courts and in villages, at
the universities and at the castles. And everyone acted
so splendidly! And their one common goal? To show
themselves, reveal their true souls...

SECOND
(In mommy-speak.) Waldy, you're still in the nude,

Hurry up, you'll be late to school!

THIRD
Waldemeryu, God will punish you...

SECOND
Lead the dance, in pairs!

THIRD
Walde! Love me if you dare...

SECOND
But, of course, ma'am, with much flair...
(Pause.) Walde, love me with some guts!

THIRD
But, ma'am, only if I must.
(Pause.) Walde, love me with an ease!

SECOND
Can you, ma'am, ever be pleased...

FIRST
(Pensive.) The magic of theatre does not come from
superficial dress-ups and the like, but from its depth, and
from what it can reveal. *(Loud.)* Curtain up! We reveal
a human being! He was hiding behind it, but now, we
have him here, in front of us. Here he is: the misanthrope,
don quixote, hero, imaginary invalid, Othello, Hamlet,
Mefisto...

THIRD
Oh, Waldi, my dear, let me go for God's sake,
What you do, I can no longer take.

SECOND
(On the side.) Waldo, set the women free,
If you don't want to get beat up by me.

FIRST
I dream of a theatre of the fourth dimension. Ha! A
theatre without label that the audiences like so much.
Expressionism! Ach, we know, we know. You know
nothing! Theatre, real theatre cannot be labeled. Call me
what you like it, but you won't leave the building calm
and rested! You'll be thinking about what you've just seen
for a long time, which doesn't happen every day, you must
admit. Normally, you leave and you forget. Like from a
loo! Theatre is not a loo, remember this, you, the audience
member who likes to get his hands wet...

SECOND
(Interrupting him.) Liked to get his hands wet!
Waldy, let us into the toil-let.

THIRD
Wait, let me zip my pants,
While unzipped I cannot prance!

FIRST
Let's excommunicate everyone who doesn't love theatre!
We are the lunatics of the truth. Lunatics, I'm telling you.
The moon...

THIRD
Waldi, the moon's rising in the night sky.

SECOND
So, let it rise, rise and shine...
You smell as you live...
We're young at heart, and that's it!

FIRST
I don't want to see everyday life. That's a price your soul
has to pay for its freedom. Because the soul is free! At the
theatre...

SECOND
*(Interrupts the FIRST, but he is not saying anything, just opens
his mouth.)* ...I can't think of anything else to say. *(To
FIRST.)* I was waiting for you to finish, while we've played
around with made-up nursery rhymes. So, what, are we
getting back to work?

THIRD
Waldemare... *(Nothing.)*

FIRST
(To THIRD.) I like you.

THIRD
(Embarrassed, doesn't know what to say.) A...

FIRST
I like you, but this scene needs to be more expressive.
With your talent, it shouldn't be difficult to do. And talent
you've got, that's for sure.

SECOND
I've got talent too!

FIRST
I don't know, I just don't know. If I were you, I wouldn't
be so sure of it.

SECOND
(Reaching into his pocket.) I can show you the reviews. Do
you know what the critics wrote about me?

FIRST
I don't know and I don't want to know. You need to focus
and act out what you need to act out, with some zest and
zeal…

SECOND
I'm not a seal.

FIRST
It's an expression. Do I have to explain everything to you?

SECOND
(Eager.) Yes. Please, explain everything to me. I'd be
happy to listen. I'm an excellent listener. Your friend,
the director – you know who I'm talking about – used to
explain everything to us. And we've listened to him.

FIRST
But, that's exactly what I'm doing right now: explaining it
to you. You have to act with zest and zeal. Enigmatically
and outrageously; the way for the viewer to see the real
you. You can do it this way. You have a range…

THIRD
Are we acting or flirting? Flirting I can have at a picnic.
We're supposed to do theatre here, for Goodness sake…

FIRST
One more time: calmly, but neurotically, focused and discombobulated at the same time, get it?

SECOND and THIRD
(Speaking together.)

THIRD
What costumes will we wear?

FIRST
What costumes?

THIRD
We are the ones asking you the question! *(THIRD and SECOND leave slowly, talking lazily with the FIRST.)*

FIRST
There won't be any costumes. Just everyday clothes, tuxedos, bowties.

SECOND
Tuxedos and bowties are not everyday clothes. A dirty sweater, dirty because everything's dirty and I only have one wife – and she has not studied to be a laundress – a dirty sweater, that's a piece of everyday clothing.

FIRST
You wouldn't be able to act it out wearing a sweater. It would be unbelievable, untheatrical.

THIRD
(From farther away.) Elegant suit and a hat.

FIRST
You'll look like a gangster.

SECOND
A gangster is a man too.

THIRD
A man lives and dies.

SECOND
That's why I say, wash yourself.

THIRD and SECOND leave.

THIRD
I would, if I could.
(Pause.) A sweater covers, a sweater protects.

SECOND
You're a dumb piece of shit!

FIRST
Stop it! Stop these nursery rhymes! We'll never finish what we're supposed to finish. We have to rethink everything thoughtfully. Thoughtless play is a nightmare!

THIRD
You should have told us this from the start. We wouldn't have wasted so much time.

FIRST
Tuxedo, bowtie, dress shoes. That's a good look for you. Don't dry your hands on your butt, as you usually do it. You can't do it wearing a tuxedo. You shouldn't do it when you're not wearing a tuxedo, but when you're wearing a tuxedo, you really shouldn't do it. They're supposed to be two gentlemen, not over sophisticated, but elegant. Otherwise, it will be too confusing.

THIRD
You think so? *(From far away.)*

FIRST
I'm sure of that. *(To himself, since the other two have left.)* I'm sure of that. I'm not sure of other things, but I'm sure of that. *(Alone and silent for a long while. Suddenly.)* Ha! He had it coming! Every idiot wants to outshine every other idiot! Stun everyone with his brilliance, no matter what! Great artist, he is, right! He invites a mob – excuse me, the audience – and makes a happening! And when I ask him, **what** is it exactly that he's doing, he replies that

he doesn't know yet, but it will *come* to him at the last minute! It will come to him! What can possibly *come* to that moron! He says: Oh, I don't need a director, it's not theatre. It's a situation, which will just *come to him, come* out. Come out! To him! *(Takes a pause and calms himself.)* A director is needed even for the simplest, dumbest things. School recitals, fashion shows, even funerals! Of course, I'm not pushy. I just want to help. He's too dumb to even know he needs a good director. *(Continues...)* Chaos and confusion will come out! Shit will come out!

The audience will finally realize that the FIRST is reciting the same text he has recited at the opening of the play. He was then standing in the same pose, making the same gestures, and waiting for the other two to come over.